GOVERNING CLIMATE CHANGE

Governing Climate Change, Second Edition provides a short and accessible introduction to how climate change is governed by an increasingly diverse range of actors, from civil society and market actors to multilateral development banks, donors, and cities.

This updated edition also includes:

- up-to-date coverage of the negotiations post-Copenhagen (Cancún, Durban, and towards Paris) and some of the shifts in the inter-governmental politics;
- a deeper discussion of the roles of actors that have come to prominence in the climate negotiations;
- an overview of key funding mechanisms such as the Green Climate Fund, Adaptation Fund, the High-Level Advisory Group on Climate Change Finance, and REDD (Reducing Emissions from Deforestation and forest Degradation);
- a direct assessment of what the proliferation of TCCG (Transnational Climate Change Governance) adds up to in terms of legitimacy, effectiveness etc., drawing on all the recent research in this area;
- an analysis of renewable energy in the UK (in the light of recent controversies around the siting of wind turbines and fracking projects).

Providing an interdisciplinary perspective drawing on geography, politics, international relations, and development studies, this book is essential reading for students and scholars concerned not only with climate governance but also with the future of the environment in general.

Harriet Bulkeley is a Professor in the Department of Geography at Durham University. Her research interests are in the nature and politics of environmental governance with a focus on climate change and urban sustainability.

Peter Newell is Professor in the Department of International Relations at the University of Sussex. He works on the political economy of energy and climate change.

ROUTLEDGE GLOBAL INSTITUTIONS SERIES

Edited by Thomas G. Weiss
The CUNY Graduate Center, New York, USA
and Rorden Wilkinson
University of Sussex, Brighton, UK

ABOUT THE SERIES

The "Global Institutions Series" provides cutting-edge books about many aspects of what we know as "global governance." It emerges from our shared frustrations with the state of available knowledge—electronic and print-wise, for research and teaching—in the area. The series is designed as a resource for those interested in exploring issues of international organization and global governance. And since the first volumes appeared in 2005, we have taken significant strides toward filling conceptual gaps.

The series consists of three related "streams" distinguished by their blue, red, and green covers. The blue volumes, comprising the majority of the books in the series, provide user-friendly and short (usually no more than 50,000 words) but authoritative guides to major global and regional organizations, as well as key issues in the global governance of security, the environment, human rights, poverty, and humanitarian action among others. The books with red covers are designed to present original research and serve as extended and more specialized treatments of issues pertinent for advancing understanding about global governance. And the volumes with green covers—the most recent departure in the series—are comprehensive and accessible accounts of the major theoretical approaches to global governance and international organization.

The books in each of the streams are written by experts in the field, ranging from the most senior and respected authors to first-rate scholars at the beginning of their careers. In combination, the three components of the series—blue, red, and green—serve as key resources for faculty, students, and practitioners alike. The works in the blue and green streams have value as core and complementary readings in courses on, among other things, international organization, global governance, international law, international relations, and international political economy; the red volumes allow further reflection and investigation in these and related areas.

The books in the series also provide a segue to the foundation volume that offers the most comprehensive textbook treatment available dealing with all the major issues, approaches, institutions, and actors in contemporary global governance—our edited work *International Organization and Global Governance* (2014) a volume to which many of the authors in the series have contributed essays.

Understanding global governance—past, present, and future—is far from a finished journey. The books in this series nonetheless represent significant steps toward a better way of conceiving contemporary problems and issues as well as, hopefully, doing something to improve world order. We value the feedback from our readers and their role in helping shape the on-going development of the series.

A complete list of titles appears at the end of this book. The most recent titles in the series are:

Representing Islam in International Relations (2015)
by Turan Kayaoglu

Contemporary Human Rights Ideas (2nd edition, 2015)
by Bertrand G. Ramcharan

The Politics of International Organizations (2015)
edited by Patrick Weller and Xu Yi-chong

Global Poverty (2nd edition, 2015)
by David Hulme

Global Corporations and Global Governance (2015)
by Christopher May

The United Nations Centre on Transnational Corporations (2015)
by Khalil Hamdani and Lorraine Ruffing

The Challenges of Constructing Legitimacy in Peacebuilding (2015)
by Daisaku Higashi

Bulkeley and Newell have updated their *Governing Climate Change* with coverage of the many new developments in climate governance, without losing any of the sharpness, concision, and breadth of coverage of their excellent first edition of the book. It will be core reading for anyone trying to understand the bewildering complexity of how societies are trying to grapple with climate change.

Matthew Paterson, *Professor of Political Science, University of Ottawa, Canada*

Praise for the previous edition:
In *Governing Climate Change*, two of Britain's leading experts offer a comprehensive yet accessible study on current climate policy, with a highly refreshing and innovative look at the vast universe of politics beyond the state. Newell and Bulkeley's powerful analysis shows convincingly that climate governance reaches much farther than the traditional intergovernmental regime.

Frank Biermann, *Professor of Political Science and of Environmental Policy Sciences, Vrije Universiteit Amsterdam, The Netherlands*

GOVERNING CLIMATE CHANGE

Second Edition

Harriet Bulkeley and
Peter Newell

LONDON AND NEW YORK

First published 2015
by Routledge
2 Park Square, Milton Park, Abingdon, Oxon OX14 4RN

and by Routledge
711 Third Avenue, New York, NY 10017

Routledge is an imprint of the Taylor & Francis Group, an informa business

British Library Cataloguing in Publication Data
A catalogue record for this book is available from the British Library

Library of Congress Cataloging in Publication Data

Bulkeley, Harriet, 1972–
Governing climate change / Harriet Bulkeley and Peter Newell. – 2nd edition.
pages cm. – (Routledge global institutions series ; 104)
Includes bibliographical references and index.
1. Climatic changes–Government policy–International cooperation. I. Newell, Peter (Peter John) II. Title.

QC903.B85 2015
363.738'74–dc23
2014046799

ISBN: 978-1-138-79570-9 (hbk)
ISBN: 978-1-138-79571-6 (pbk)
ISBN: 978-1-315-75823-7 (ebk)

Typeset in Times New Roman
by Sunrise Setting Ltd, Paignton, UK

Printed and bound in the United States of America by Publishers Graphics, LLC on sustainably sourced paper.

CONTENTS

LIST OF FIGURES AND BOXES

Figures

Boxes

ABOUT THE AUTHORS

Harriet Bulkeley is a Professor in the Department of Geography at Durham University. Her research interests are in the nature and politics of environmental governance with a focus on climate change and urban sustainability. She is co-author of *An Urban Politics of Climate Change* (with Vanesa Castán Broto and Gareth Edwards) (2014) and *Transnational Climate Change Governance* (with the Leverhulme Transnational Climate Change Governance Network) (2014), and co-editor (with Johannes Stripple) of *Governing the Climate* (2014).

Peter Newell is Professor of International Relations and former Director of the Centre for Global Political Economy at the University of Sussex. His research is currently focussed on the political economy of low carbon energy transitions. He is author of *Climate for Change* (2000); co-author (with Matthew Paterson) of *Climate Capitalism* (2010), *Transnational Climate Change Governance* (with the Leverhulme Transnational Climate Change Governance Network) (2014); and co-editor of *The New Carbon Economy* (with Emily Boyd and Max Boykoff) (2012).

ABBREVIATIONS

3C	Combat Climate Change
ABARE	Australian Bureau of Agriculture and Resource Economics
ADP	Ad Hoc Working Group on the Durban Platform for Enhanced Action
AGBM	Ad Hoc Group on the Berlin Mandate
AIJ	activities implemented jointly
AOSIS	Alliance of Small Island States
APP	Asia Pacific Partnership on Clean Development and Climate
BRICS	Brazil, Russia, India, China, and South Africa
C40	C40 Climate Leadership Group
CAN	Climate Action Network
CBDP	community-based disaster preparedness
CCB	climate, community and biodiversity
CCBA	Climate Community and Biodiversity Alliance
CCI	Clinton Climate Initiative
CCP	Cities for Climate Protection
cCR	carbonn Cities Climate Registry
CCX	Chicago Climate Exchange
CDCF	Community Development Carbon Fund
CDM	Clean Development Mechanism
CDP	Carbon Disclosure Project
CERES	Coalition for Environmentally Responsible Economies
CERs	certified emissions reductions
CIFs	Climate Investment Funds
CIFOR	Center for International Forestry Research

CO_2	carbon dioxide
CO_2e	carbon dioxide equivalent
COP	Conference of the Parties
CSR	corporate social responsibility
DEFRA	Department for Environment and Rural Affairs
DNV	Det Norske Veritas
EC	European Commission
ECLAC	Economic Commission for Latin America and the Caribbean
ECO	Environmental Conservation Organization
ERT	European Round Table of Industrialists
ETS	Emissions Trading Scheme
EU	European Union
FIT	feed-in-tariff
FIELD	Foundation for International Environmental Law and Development
G77	group of developing countries (originally 77 that signed a declaration in 1964)
G8	Group of Eight
GCC	Global Climate Coalition
GDP	gross domestic product
GEF	Global Environment Facility
GHG	greenhouse gases
GRILA	Group of Latin American countries
HSBC	Hong Kong and Shanghai Banking Corporation
ICC	Inuit Circumpolar Conference
ICCR	Interfaith Centre for Corporate Responsibility
ICLEI	Local Governments for Sustainability
ICSU	International Council for Science (formerly International Council of Scientific Unions)
IETA	International Emissions Trading Association
IFC	International Finance Corporation
IIED	International Institute for Environment and Development
IMF	International Monetary Fund
IPCC	Intergovernmental Panel on Climate Change
ISO	International Organization for Standardization
JI	joint implementation
JUSCANZ	Japan, US, Canada, Australia, and New Zealand
LDCs	least developed countries

LDF	local development framework
LULUCF	land use, land-use change, and forestry
mCHP	micro combined heat and power
NEG-ECP	New England Governors and Eastern Canadian Premiers
NGOs	non-governmental organizations
nrg4SD	Network of Regional Governments for Sustainable Development
ODA	Official Development Assistance
OECD	Organization for Economic Cooperation and Development
OPEC	Organization of Petroleum Exporting Countries
PCF	Prototype Carbon Fund
PPP	public–private partnerships
PRA	participatory rapid appraisal
PSA-CABSA	Payments for Carbon, Biodiversity and Agro-forestry services
PV	photovoltaics
QELROs	quantifiable emissions limitations and reduction obligations
REDD	Reducing Emissions from Deforestation and forest Degradation
REEEP	Renewable Energy and Energy Efficiency Partnership
SBI	Subsidiary Body for Implementation
SBSTA	Subsidiary Body for Scientific and Technological Advice
SGS	Société Générale de Surveillance
TCCG	Transnational Climate Change Governance
TCG	The Climate Group
TT	Transition Towns
UK	United Kingdom
UN	United Nations
UNCED	United Nations Conference on Environment and Development
UNDP	United Nations Development Programme
UNEP	United Nations Environment Programme
UNFCCC	United Nations Framework Convention on Climate Change

UNICE	Union of Industrial Employers' Confederations in Europe (now Business Europe)
UNIDO	United Nations Industrial Development Organization
US	United States of America
VCA	Vulnerability and Capacity Assessment
VCS	Verified Carbon Standard
WBCSD	World Business Council on Sustainable Development
WOCoRe	West Oxford Community Renewables
WMO	World Meteorological Organization
WRI	World Resources Institute
WRM	World Rainforest Movement
WSSD	World Summit on Sustainable Development
WTO	World Trade Organization
WWF	World Wide Fund for Nature

ACKNOWLEDGEMENTS

Both authors would like to thank the series editor Rorden Wilkinson for proposing the idea of a second edition of the book, and the publishing team at Routledge, and especially Peter Harris, for their assistance with producing the book. They would also like to express their gratitude to Andrea Brock for research assistance in the preparation of the final manuscript.

Harriet Bulkeley would like to thank Peter Newell for inviting her to be involved with this project, and for being a committed and thought-provoking co-author. She is also thankful for the love and support of Peter Matthews, which continue to sustain her work and life.

Peter Newell would like to express his gratitude to Harriet Bulkeley for being a willing, efficient and engaging co-author. He would like to show his appreciation for the love and support of Lucila throughout this and many other ventures.

The book is dedicated to our respective children Elodie, Thea, Ana and Camilo for whom the question of the effectiveness of climate governance is of much more than academic interest.

Harriet Bulkeley and Peter Newell
October 2014

INTRODUCTION
Governing climate change

Climate change is one of the most pressing scientific and political challenges of our time. With almost daily news reports of climate-related disasters, international meetings, scientific findings, and various forms of protest, it is unsurprising that the issue is both at the top of the international political agenda and one of significant public interest. Over the past 25 years, we have witnessed the perhaps paradoxical twin processes of growing scientific certainty about the causes and consequences of climate change, and rising concern that the issue presents an intractable problem for global governance. While the reports from the Intergovernmental Panel on Climate Change (IPCC) have built an increasingly alarming picture of the changes that increased levels of greenhouse gases (GHG) in the atmosphere may precipitate, the international community has been slow to take proportionate action. In this book, we examine the governance of climate change in order to understand why and how the issue is being addressed and by whom, and to explore the challenges which arise from attempting to confront such a serious threat to our collective well-being.

In this introductory chapter, we consider why conventional accounts of international cooperation and efforts to address the issue may fail to provide a sufficient account of the contemporary landscape of climate governance. We develop an alternative approach, which goes beyond existing thinking about global governance, to help us to understand why, how, and by whom climate change is being governed, and with what consequences.

The governance challenge

Before we consider what different theoretical perspectives might have to say about the nature of climate change governance, it is appropriate to look at the problem itself in more detail. In particular, we suggest that the complexity of governing climate change stems from three related factors: the multiple scales of political decision making involved; the fragmented and blurred roles of state and non-state actors; and the deeply embedded nature of many of the processes that lead to emissions of GHG in everyday processes of production and consumption.[1]

Turning first to the issue of the scale of the climate change problem, it is commonly assumed that climate change is a "global problem." If we take a closer look at this assumption, however, we can see that the very nature of how "global" is interpreted can lead to radically different understandings of where, and with whom, the challenge of addressing climate change lies. For some, the global nature of climate change comes from the physical nature of the problem—because GHG emissions know no boundaries; emissions in one place and time contribute to increasing atmospheric concentrations, which in turn will have impacts across the globe. Because no one country can tackle climate change alone, addressing climate change needs a global solution—usually interpreted as cooperation between nation-states—in order to reduce emissions worldwide and prevent the problem of free-riding, of some benefiting from the actions of others. This understanding of the climate change problem has become orthodox, and the challenge of governing climate change globally is frequently assumed to be that of agreeing cooperation, normally in the form of an international treaty, among the relevant nation-states. In effect, this leads to an understanding of climate change as an inter-national problem since states are the primary participants in international institutions and have the authority to sign up to international accords. There are, however, alternative means through which the global nature of climate change could be understood. For example, one approach would be to consider the global processes through which emissions of GHG are generated—flows of production, trade, and consumption, for example—which would signal a very different geography of responsibility, suggesting that multinational corporations and consumers had a more significant role to play in reducing emissions of GHG than the countries in which particular goods were produced.[2] One example of this kind of global geography of climate change can be found in the study by Greenpeace International that compared the carbon dioxide (CO_2) emissions from the burning of fossil fuels by major oil companies with those of certain countries, and found that Shell emits more than Saudi Arabia, Amoco more than Canada, Mobil more than Australia, and BP, Exxon, and Texaco more than France, Spain, and the Netherlands.[3] Another study by the Climate Accountability Institute found that "63% of cumulative worldwide emissions of industrial CO_2 and methane between 1751 and 2010" could be traced to 90 major economic actors in the fossil fuel and cement industries, with half of these emissions having been produced since 1986 (see Figure I.1).[4] Hence, if we think of global as a causal rather than a spatial category (particularly one bounded by the borders of a nation-state), we are directed to a very different starting point for thinking about who governs climate change and where that governing takes place.

At the same time, the very framing of climate change as a global problem tends to neglect other scales of decision making which shape the trajectories of GHG emissions and the potential to adapt to climate change. Rather than conceiving of climate change as a global problem, many scholars now suggest it needs to be considered as a multilevel problem, in which different levels of decision making—local, regional, national, and international—as well as new spheres and arenas of governance that cut across such boundaries are involved in both creating and addressing climate change.[5] Indeed we show throughout the book how actors operating at all these levels are involved in the governance of climate change.

FIGURE I.1   Whose carbon is it?

Source: Carbon Majors available online at http://carbonmajors.org/more-downloadable-graphics-for-carbon-majors-study/ [accessed January 15, 2015].

Opening up the framing of climate change as an international problem also leads to questions about the role of nation-states in its governance. The focus of many analyses of climate change has been on what nation-states, collectively and individually, are or are not doing to combat the issue. This is clearly important—nation-states have significant power and influence over many of the processes which contribute to climate change and reduce vulnerability. However, it is increasingly recognized that nation-states are also limited in the degree to which they can directly affect emissions of GHG and the ability of societies and economies to adapt to climate change. While the language of international agreements and national policy documents often suggests that nation-states can act as containers for emissions of GHG—cutting up the global emissions pie into nation-sized pieces, setting targets, and conducting emissions inventories—the GHG emitted within the boundaries of a nation-state are shaped by processes and actors operating across national boundaries, and moreover, only partially within the purview of the state itself. As Geoffrey Heal argues:

> carbon dioxide is produced as a result of billions of de-centralized and independent decisions by private households for heating and transportation and by corporations for these and other needs, all outside the government sphere. The government can influence these decisions, but only indirectly through regulations or incentives.[6]

In part, this reflects the changing nature of the state in the current era of globalization and neo-liberal economic reform. So that whereas some nation-states may once have been able to exercise sovereign authority over those sectors where emissions of GHG are concentrated, such as energy, transport, and agriculture, others have never enjoyed a monopoly of power in these sectors. In many cases, however, the nature of the economic and political interests at work is shifting in response to the globalization of investment, development, and ownership of infrastructure and utility assets. For example, many energy markets have been liberalized and privatized, leaving the nation-state with little influence over the generation and supply of energy,[7] and even countries such as South Africa that managed to resist some of the power sector reforms that have been applied elsewhere in Africa are gradually opening up their energy markets to foreign and private independent power producers.[8] At the same time, a globalized economy makes many governments wary of introducing policies such as taxation,[9] when businesses threatened with such measures can relocate to areas of the world where there is less or virtually no regulation of their emissions. This means that nation-states have to engage in forms of negotiation and cooperation with non-state actors as they are increasingly dependent on them for realizing their objectives through public–private partnerships (PPP) and other arrangements.[10] Any analytical framework that seeks to understand how climate change is governed therefore needs to recognize the range of actors that are now involved in the processes of governing climate change.

The critical involvement of non-state actors in climate governance partly reflects a third key feature of the issue—the economically and socially embedded nature of the production of GHG emissions. Unlike other global environmental issues, such as ozone depletion, the causes of which were relatively confined to one industrial sector based largely in Europe and North America, or rainforest destruction, which is confined to specific geographic locations, climate change stems from a complex range of processes, cutting across place and scale, which are deeply embedded in our current ways of living. As Timothy Mitchell argues, "the concentration of energy supplies in large amounts at specific sites led to the creation of an apparatus of energy supply with which the democratic politics of the late nineteenth and early twentieth centuries would be built."[11] Given that the use of energy is at the heart of modern life and central to achieving economic growth, carving out a specific terrain for climate change governance is problematic both in terms of containing the scope of international and national policy, and also because decisions reached in other domains—concerning trade, energy security, and infrastructure planning to name just a few—will have critical implications for the success or otherwise of efforts for governing climate change.

The multiscale, multiactor, and embedded nature of the issue poses significant challenges for how we understand and analyze climate change governance. In this book, we develop a new approach to address these challenges. First, we seek to move away from the idea that climate change is exclusively a global issue—an emphasis which implies a narrow focus upon public international policy—and instead to understand the shifting terrain of climate governance across different scales and networks. Second, we shift away from the position that the nation-state is the only or necessarily most important unit of climate politics to consider the other actors involved, and the ways in which public and private authority operate in climate governance.[12] This involves rethinking where responsibility for addressing climate change might lie, and raises interesting questions about who the relevant actors are in governing climate change, how and why they govern climate change the way they do, and with what implications. Third, we suggest that conventional understandings of rights, risks, and responsibilities assume a narrow view of who wields power and exercises agency in global climate politics which serve to reproduce a restrictive emphasis on reducing emissions through state pledges rather than promoting the de-carbonization of the processes and services which generate GHG,[13] which are often diffuse, transnational, and frequently beyond direct state control as we saw above. Before we set out this approach, let us first look in more detail at existing and conventional approaches to explaining the governance of climate change and the critiques that have emerged.

Climate change: an international problem?

As we outlined above, approaches to understanding climate change as an international problem commonly start with the fact that the atmosphere, in contrast to the world of states, knows no boundaries. Emissions of GHG in one place at one time can have impacts which stretch over time and space in complex ways. Those who have made little or no contribution to the problem will also suffer its consequences, and often it is the most vulnerable who have the least culpability. Managing climate change, from this perspective, entails managing a problem of a resource held in common, over which no one institution or actor has control. In a classic framing of the problem, Andrew Hurrell puts it:

> Can a fragmented and often highly conflictual political system made up of over 170 sovereign states and numerous other actors achieve the high (and historically unprecedented) levels of cooperation and policy coordination needed to manage environmental problems on a global scale?[14]

As with other areas in which international cooperation is required, scholars have sought to understand the politics of climate change through the deployment of regime approaches which seek to explain the creation, stability, and effectiveness of international institutions and the agreements they oversee (see Box I.1).[15] These perspectives proved particularly attractive for understanding the dynamics of international climate change politics since they respond "to a number of overlapping concerns" that "traditionally characterize the global environmental problematic."[16] These include the desire to regulate states' behavior in order to avoid the so-called tragedy of commons, the need to control tendencies towards free-riding, and the need to respond to the distributive questions arising from the collective response to global environmental challenges. Across a broad body of work concerned with understanding the conditions under which nation-states co-operate to address international problems, there are significant differences in terms of understanding the processes through which regimes are created and operate. Here, we consider three different perspectives and examine the insights that they bring to understanding the process of governing climate change, before considering their shortcomings in the light of the challenges of the climate governance problem raised above.

BOX I.1 DEFINING A REGIME

International regimes are "social institutions that consist of agreed upon principles, norms, rules, decision making procedures, and programs that govern the interactions of actors in specific issue areas."

Source: Oran Young, "Rights, Rules and Resources in World Affairs," in *Global Governance: Drawing Insights from the Environmental Experience*, ed. Oran Young (Cambridge, Mass.: MIT Press, 1997), 5–6.

Understanding regimes

In power-based accounts of regimes, regimes are formed and dominated by a hegemon, the nation-state with the most (economic and military) power which it can use either to promote cooperation or forestall international agreement.[17] Powerful states can either use their resources and power to create and finance regimes out of an enlightened self-interest in a well-governed international system, such as the United States did with the creation of the World Bank and International Monetary Fund (IMF) at the end of the Second World War, or, by contrast, exercise a veto role by withdrawing their support for a regime or just ignoring it.[18] Here, the design of international institutions is less important than the motivations of the hegemon, and the distribution of power in the international system, in terms of the outcome of the regime. In the case of climate change, as in many other issue areas, scholars have pointed to the United States as a potential hegemon.[19] As we discuss in further detail in Chapter 2, initially, the United States took part in the development of the international agreements for addressing climate change—the United Nations Framework Convention on Climate Change (UNFCCC) and the Kyoto Protocol—but withdrew from Kyoto in 2001. On the one hand, the ability of the United States to withdraw from such an agreement on a high profile issue points to the fragility of regimes and their dependence on the will of the most powerful state.[20] On the other hand, the survival of Kyoto, despite the withdrawal of the United States, and the rapprochement between the Obama administration and the climate change regime suggest that international institutions are more than the sum of their (powerful) parts. Perhaps more fundamentally, scholars have questioned the basis upon which power is conceived within such approaches. The assumption that interests are predetermined and materially based (on economic wealth or military might) has been challenged in the context of environmental issues that are inherently uncertain and in which interests are difficult to discern at the outset of negotiations.[21] We return to this point below.

A second set of approaches for understanding regimes is also concerned with the role of interests in shaping international cooperation. Unlike power-based approaches, functionalist or interest-based accounts of regimes are concerned with how different institutional designs shape and affect the behavior of nation-states.[22] Interest-based accounts suggest that, over the long term:

> regimes are formed when state actors perceive that individual actions with respect to a given issue-area will not promote their interests in the long run. Regimes, here, are seen as the medium used by state actors to reduce vulnerability, opportunism, and uncertainty while stabilizing the expectations needed to promote collective action.[23]

The focus is on the ability of institutions to reduce transaction costs, share information, and enable communication, and so build trust and provide a shadow of the future; a sense that short-term engagement will pay long-term dividends. Hence, from this perspective, many of the disincentives to cooperate that power-based approaches emphasize are addressed by the ability of institutions to build cooperation through trust, bargaining, and the careful design of institutions which can deter free-riders.

In a third approach to understanding regimes, the emphasis is shifted away from rationalist and interest-based accounts to consider the roles of norms, values, and knowledge in shaping the positions adopted by nation-states and the evolution of international institutions. These constructivist accounts focus on "international regimes as a means through which cognitive and normative aspects of the problem in question come to be constructed and learnt, and in turn shape the ways in which states perceive their interests."[24] By opening up the question of how nation-states come to have interests, and how these evolve, constructivist accounts widen the temporal and spatial horizons of regime theory by including prenegotiation phases of interest development, domestic processes through which interests come to be conceived, and a range of non-state actors involved in developing norms and knowledge about the nature of the climate change problem and how it should be governed.[25] One key aspect of this work has been to point to the role of scientific knowledge in shaping the international politics of climate change through the role of epistemic communities, who "are both politically empowered through their claims to exercise authoritative knowledge and motivated by shared causal and principled beliefs."[26] The IPCC could be regarded as fulfilling the criteria for an epistemic community, with a shared understanding of the causal processes involved in climatic change, normative beliefs (e.g. in a precautionary approach), common tests for the validity of knowledge (e.g. the extensive processes of peer review involved in IPCC reports), and a common policy project based on the need to reduce emissions of GHG.[27] However, whether and how this consensual knowledge has influenced the development of the climate change regime is less clear. While the IPCC was regarded as playing a critical role in the early stages of the development of the regime, once negotiations began their influence can be seen to have diminished. For example, the IPCC has regularly stated that reductions in GHG emissions in the order of 60 percent of 1990 levels by 2050 are needed in industrialized countries. At Kyoto, a collective target of 5 percent reductions by 2010 was agreed, which is rather far removed from the scientific consensus. As Paterson argues:

> it was clearly not the case that an epistemic consensus neatly produced international cooperation on the climate issue. Instead, it produced resources for policymakers from different countries (or from within different parts of the state within those countries) to advance the positions they preferred—it became another strategic argument at their disposal. Thus, oil producing countries were able to emphasize the uncertainties (even those within the limits of the scientific consensus).[28]

As we discuss in more depth in Chapter 2, rather than a process in which consensual science is unproblematically translated into policy action, the relation between science and climate policy is complex and deeply politicized.[29] This issue points to a wider problem with constructivist approaches. The focus on knowledge and norms can belie the fragile and contested process through which interests are forged, and overlook other important material and political factors that shape the positions taken by different actors which reduces their explanatory power in relation to the governance of climate change.

Critiques

Regime approaches have provided powerful tools for understanding and analyzing the politics of climate change at the global level. We have shown how different accounts of regimes have demonstrated the roles of powerful states, international institutions, non-state actors, and structural factors in shaping the international climate negotiations and policy outcomes. However, we find that regime approaches are also limited in their scope, particularly with respect to the key challenges of climate change as an environmental problem—the multiple scales and actors involved, and the close integration between the causes and consequences of climate change, economic development, and everyday life. Here, we highlight four critiques of regime approaches which we suggest restrict its analytical power for understanding the governance of climate change.

The first issue concerns where the governance of climate change is seen to take place. In keeping with orthodox accounts of the global nature of climate change, which we discussed at the start of this chapter, regime approaches tend to assume that the location of climate change as a governance problem is in a discrete political domain which we can label "the global." As a consequence, different levels of governance—notably domestic and international arenas—remain treated for the most part as distinct. While some scholars have sought to understand the interplay, or interaction, between different levels of governance—and the interaction between, for example, domestic and international politics[30]—this model of hierarchical, discrete scales underplays both the fluidity of interaction at such frontiers as well as how many of the processes that cause climate change operate across these boundaries.[31]

The second issue relates to who is regarded as conducting the governance of climate change. Regime approaches continue to take "as given the preeminent status of the nation-states as the key point of reference in seeking account for the ways issued unfold in the global agenda."[32] While some accounts acknowledge the role of non-state actors, their function is primarily determined with respect to how they have sought to influence nation-states and inter-national institutions. This state-centric approach is, we think, problematic for it serves to limit our analysis of how non-state actors are involved in climate governance. Furthermore, as an entity the state remains essentially black-boxed—the nature of the state and how it operates is taken for granted, so that questions concerning how state institutions vary with historical and geographic context, and of how state power is used in practice are rarely raised. One side effect is the extension of a Western conception of the state, its capacity, and role in society as a model for states everywhere, ignoring important differences in the nature of the state across the globe.[33] Another is that the state is regarded as a neutral actor with regard to the actors and interests it is meant to regulate; an assumption which overlooks the state's dependence on economic actors, particularly in key sectors such as energy which are so central to all other industries, and the structural power that this confers on business actors to shape the context in which states make decisions about which courses of action are desirable and possible.[34]

The third issue concerns how climate governance takes place. Insofar as it is considered explicitly at all, climate governance is conceived as a top-down process, implemented through international agreements, national policies, and various forms of market instrument. It is assumed that this happens in a cascade fashion in which decisions and authority flow downwards from one level to the next in a linear way.[35] While different traditions of regime theory offer alternative explanations for such processes—whether they be rationally based or driven by new norms or knowledge—little attention is paid to the actual practices through which policies and measures are achieved and which other actors are implicated in this process, and the implications of this for what is and is not included in the remit of climate governance.

Finally, we suggest that regime approaches have to date failed to provide sufficient insights as to why climate governance is taking place, and indeed to the particular form that it takes. While explanations are offered in terms of the power of individual actors, institutions, or norms, such approaches work with a particular concept of power which regards it as a force exercised by some actors over others, neglecting both the structural and generative aspects of power. On the one hand, by focusing on the power of actors and of ideas to produce particular outcomes, regime approaches tend to neglect the ways in which power operates to structure the rules of the game within which such contests occur. This in turn means that questions concerning who is served by particular arrangements or forms of governance, of who wins and who loses and why, are often ignored. On the other hand, regarding power as a discrete property of some actors implies the conceptualization of power in zero-sum terms such that, for example, "an increase in the power of non-state actors is ipsofacto defined as a simultaneous reduction on state power and authority."[36] Conceiving of power differently, as a facility to "enable things to happen,"[37] allows us to consider the way in which power is generated through the process of governing itself, and move beyond dualistic accounts of the roles of state and non-state actors in addressing climate change.

Global governance perspectives

In part as a response to concerns about the analytical power of the regime approach, scholars within the discipline of international relations have increasingly turned to the concept of governance as a means of understanding the nature of world affairs. Across the social sciences, the term governance has gained in currency as a means of understanding the changing nature of the state and the proliferation of actors and mechanisms involved in the governing of societies. In its broadest sense, governance "relates to any form of creating or maintaining political order and providing common goods for a given political community on whatever level."[38] The specific variant of this literature concerned with global governance owes much to the work of James Rosenau and his distinction between "government," confined to the world of states, and "governance," regarded as a broader phenomenon:

> Governance occurs on a global scale through both the co-ordination of states and the activities of a vast array of rule systems that exercise authority in the pursuit of goals and that function outside normal national jurisdictions. Some of the systems are formalized, many consist of essentially informal structures, and some are still largely inchoate, but taken together they cumulate to governance on a global scale.[39]

Global governance therefore encompasses the numerous activities which are significant both in establishing international rules and in shaping policy through "on-the-ground" implementation even when some such activities originate from actors that, technically speaking, "are not endowed with formal authority."[40] As Rosenau suggests, and in common with other definitions of governance, it is the involvement of non-state actors in the governing of collective affairs in particular, that sets global governance aside from other forms of international relations.

Within this broad church, several authors have identified different strands of thinking.[41] Here, we suggest that two main approaches for understanding the nature and dynamics of global governance can be discerned.[42] The first approach "resides within the realms of regime theory" where the concept of governance "has provided a way of rethinking regimes as enmeshed in broader systems of governance instead of issue areas."[43] Closest in approach and analysis to the constructivist version of regime theory, work in this vein moves beyond examining how non-state actors have influenced the positions of nation-states or international negotiations to examine the significant role of non-state actors in governing climate change within and alongside the regime. Much of this work has focused on the role of non-governmental organizations (NGOs).[44] Such organizations can adopt "insider" strategies, seeking to shape the governing of issues such as climate change through the provision of advice, knowledge, and the development of policy solutions.[45] Within the international arena, NGOs are seen to act as diplomats and "perform many of the same functions as state delegates: they represent the interests of their constituencies, they engage in information exchange, they negotiate, and they provide policy advice."[46] For example, in her analysis of the role of NGOs in the development of the Kyoto Protocol, Michele Betsill argues that it was the specialized knowledge and expertise of NGOs in the Climate Action Network (CAN) that provided them with leverage in the negotiations. However, she suggests that the influence of NGOs was not confined to the technical arena. While there was little evidence of direct influence, in the form of the uptake of particular targets or proposals made by CAN for the Kyoto Protocol, its presence made a significant difference to the overall outcome by holding the European Union (EU) to its negotiating position of a 15 percent cut in emissions of GHG by 2010 and pressuring Al Gore, then US Vice President, to take a flexible approach to target setting. These were two important ingredients in the achievement of the final outcome of Kyoto which may not have been present without the role of the NGO community.[47] In this manner, NGOs played a role independent of individual nation-states, acting with a degree of autonomous agency in shaping the international regime.

The second approach to understanding global governance moves beyond the international arena "by acknowledging the emergence of autonomous spheres of authority beyond the national/international dichotomy" and by focusing "on the complex interlinkages between different societal actors and governmental institutions."[48] Hence, rather than focus solely on the role of non-state actors in shaping international climate institutions, such as the UNFCCC and the related Kyoto Protocol, this body of global governance work considers, for example, global climate governance as consisting of "all purposeful mechanisms and measures aimed at steering social systems towards preventing, mitigating, or adapting to the risks posed by climate change."[49] One way of seeking to capture this is the idea of a "regime complex," which refers to the interactions between a multitude of international and regional institutions whose mandates, to differing degrees, touch on the issue of climate change. It embodies the idea that "There is no integrated, comprehensive regime governing efforts to limit the extent of climate change. Instead, there is a regime complex: a loosely coupled set of specific regimes."[50] Another related strand of literature has looked at the fragmentation that results from this patchwork of public and private institutions, looking at the consequences of fragmentation, how to manage it, and the conditions of its effectiveness.[51]

Finally, scholars have examined the various roles of actors from global civil society,[52] municipal and regional networks,[53] public–private partnerships,[54] and the private sector[55] in the governance of global environmental issues,[56] with an increasing interest in moving beyond single initiatives or types of actors involved in climate governance to examining the different forms of governance architecture that are being established beyond the international regime.[57] In Chapters 4, 5, and 6 we examine examples of such approaches with respect to climate change in more detail.

Critiques and prospects

If we return to the core critiques with respect to regime approaches—concerning where, by whom, how, and why climate governance takes place—we can see that despite claims to offer an alternative, global governance perspectives share many, if not all, of the same shortcomings.

In terms of where climate governance is seen to take place, perspectives from global governance offer a significant departure from regime approaches. Rather than being confined to the international arena, much of the work conducted under the banner of global governance acknowledges both the multilevel and multiarena nature of climate governance and specifically seeks to examine how the governing of climate change is taking place beyond the international regime. In this book, we follow this line of argument and seek to examine the multiple sites—from the international arena and national governments through to transnational networks and private sector projects—in which climate governance takes place.

With regard to the second issue, concerning who governs climate change, there is perhaps less distinction from regime approaches. While both perspectives on global governance extend the range of actors involved in governing climate change, for many, in particular those adopting a regime-based account of global governance, the nation-state remains the dominant force. For example, for Paul Wapner "states remain the main actors in world affairs, and their co-operative efforts to establish regimes remain the essential building blocks of global governance in environmental and other issues."[58] Furthermore, the realms of the state and the non-state are regarded as distinct and separate, leading some scholars to conclude that the rise of non-state actors in global governance must be leading to a decline of the state. This black-boxing of the state (and non-state) spheres is unhelpful for it fails to account for the relations between state/non-state actors, and the relation between public and private authority.[59]

Work in the tradition of international political economy offers a starting point for crossing such divides, bringing into focus the nature of the state, and emphasizing its intimate relation with private actors and civil society.[60] Such approaches move away from the notion that the state is either a unitary actor or occupies an autonomous social sphere. Instead, the state is conceived as a "dynamic system of strategic selectivity"[61] through which the hegemony of one social group, or historic bloc, is attained and maintained.[62] From this perspective—sometimes referred to as a neo-Gramscian approach, because of insights derived from the writings of Antonio Gramsci about the practice of hegemony—the focus is the coalitions and alliances that different actors construct to secure, challenge, or maintain their power.[63] A strong emphasis is placed on the links between production, power, and governance, so that processes of governing which ultimately seek to regulate and change forms of production, as climate governance does, have to negotiate with those who have control over that production and their resulting power and influence.[64] This approach opens up the constitution of state/non-state relations, and requires that we "think through the many ways in which power is consolidated in institutions normally considered outside of the state."[65] Such perspectives allow us to ask important questions concerning who is governing on whose behalf, and who is excluded from such processes. In the remainder of this book, we seek to deploy perspectives from political economy to help us understand who governs climate change, and with what implications.

Like regime approaches, perspectives on global governance have also been criticized for failing to pay due attention to how governing occurs. While studies of global governance are concerned with the processes through which it takes place, Sending and Neumann suggest that

> their ontology and concomitant analytical tools are not equipped to grasp the content of the processes of governance itself. Rather, studies of global governance typically focus on the changing roles and power of state and nonstate actors, and on resulting changes in the institutionalization of political authority.[66]

As a result of this focus on the shifts in power and the institutionalization of authority, questions concerning how governance is achieved in practical terms have been relatively neglected.[67] This is an important omission for, as scholars of governmentality observe, it is through such processes that certain discourses or frames of governing are made material and "certain identities and action-orientations are defined as appropriate and normal."[68] Drawing on these insights, in this book we seek to develop an understanding of how climate governance takes place, and with what implications for how the "problem" of climate change and "its solutions" are normalized within the governance arena.

A combined lack of engagement with how and by whom climate governance is being undertaken contributes to the neglect of questions concerning why it is conducted within the literatures on global governance. In the main, key concepts concerning power and authority are similar to those used within regime approaches, such that both structural and facilitative notions of power have not been used as a means of understanding why, and with what implications, the governing of climate change is taking particular forms. In the remainder of this book, we draw on these alternative notions of power in order to understand the drivers and consequences of climate governance.

Outline

Our brief discussion of regime approaches and perspectives on global governance has demonstrated that both approaches have shortcomings when it comes to explaining where, by whom, how, and why climate governance is being conducted. We have also identified prospects for taking the considerable insights generated in these bodies of work forward, acknowledging the multiscale, multiactor, and embedded nature of the climate governance challenge, by opening up our analysis of the sites of climate governance, considering the relation between state and non-state actors in terms of who is governing climate change, examining the processes through which climate governance is being achieved, and using alternative concepts of power in order to understand why, and with what consequences, climate governance is taking place. We draw on these themes throughout the remainder of the book, and return to consider their implications in our conclusions in Chapter 6.

In Chapter 1, we provide a brief outline of the history of the emergence of climate change as a global governance problem, examining the key roles played by science, North–South politics, and the growing use of market instruments in structuring the international climate regime and the possibilities for addressing the issue. Chapter 2 focuses in more detail on the conflicts that have arisen between countries in the North and South in addressing climate change, and considers in particular what the implications of climate governance have been for issues of equity. Together, these chapters provide a picture of the emergence and development of climate change as an international and national political issue, and of the resulting consequences across different policy sectors and different places.

Chapters 3, 4, and 5 examine the emergence of climate governance in a range of political sites beyond the regime and nation-state. Chapter 3 considers the growing phenomenon of transnational networks and partnerships for addressing climate change, examining how such processes of governing take place, and assessing their implications in terms of the effectiveness and equity of climate governance. Chapter 4 focuses on the emergence of "community-based" climate governance, examining its connections to international and national policy arenas and the possibilities for self-governing approaches for addressing the issue. Chapter 5 explores the role of private actors in climate governance, considering their significance in both shaping the positions of nation-states and the international regime, and in performing governance functions in their own right. These chapters demonstrate that there is a wealth of climate governance taking place outside of the formal sites of international and national climate politics, which both carry the promise of innovative solutions and also raise considerable challenges in terms of accountability, equity, and effectiveness. In Chapter 6, we conclude by summarizing our main findings and consider the key themes that have emerged through the book and what challenges they raise conceptually and politically.

Notes

1 Karena Shaw, "Climate Deadlocks: The Environmental Politics of Energy Systems," *Environmental Politics* 20, no. 5 (2011): 743–63.
2 Yda Schreuder, *The Corporate Greenhouse: Climate Change Policy in a Globalizing World* (London: Zed Books, 2009).
3 Greenpeace International, *The Oil Industry and Climate Change: A Greenpeace Briefing* (Amsterdam, the Netherlands: Greenpeace International, 1998).
4 Richard Heede, "Tracing Anthropogenic Carbon Dioxide and Methane Emissions to Fossil Fuel and Cement Producers, 1854–2010," *Climatic Change* 122, no. 1–2 (2014): 229–41.
5 Michele Betsill and Harriet Bulkeley, "Transnational Networks and Global Environmental Governance: The Cities for Climate Protection Program," *International Studies Quarterly* 48 (2004): 471–93; John Vogler, "Taking Institutions Seriously: How Regimes Can be Relevant to Multilevel Environmental Governance," *Global Environmental Politics* 3, no. 2 (2003): 25–39; Neil Adger and Andrew Jordan, eds, *Governing Sustainability* (Cambridge: Cambridge University Press, 2009).

6 Geoffrey Heal, "New Strategies for the Provision of Global Public Goods: Learning from International Environmental Challenges," in *Global Public Goods: International Cooperation in the Twenty-first Century*, eds Inge Kaul, Isabelle Grunberg, and Marc Stern (Oxford: Oxford University Press, 1999), 240–64.

7 Adrian Smith, "Energy Governance: the Challenges of Sustainability," in *Energy for the Future: A New Agenda*, eds Ivan Scrase and Godron MacKeron (Basingstoke, UK: Palgrave, 2009), 54–76.

8 Lucy Baker, Peter Newell, and Jon Phillips, "The Political Economy of Energy Transitions: The Case of South Africa," *New Political Economy* 19, no. 6 (2014): 791–818.

9 Peter Newell and Matthew Paterson, "A Climate for Business: Global Warming, the State and Capital," *Review of International Political Economy* 5, no. 4 (1998): 679–704.

10 Phillip Pattberg, "Public Private Partnerships in Global Climate Governance," *WIREs Climate Change* 1 (2010): 279–87.

11 Timothy Mitchell, *Carbon Democracy: Political Power in the Age of Oil* (New York: Verso, 2011), 19.

12 Philipp Pattberg and Johannes Stripple, "Beyond the Public and Private Divide: Remapping Transnational Climate Governance in the 21st Century," *International Environmental Agreements: Politics, Law and Economics* 8, no. 4 (2008): 367–88.

13 *Getting Beyond the Climate Crunch: Re-thinking Rights, Risks and Responsibilities* (ESRC Briefing, 2014).

14 Andrew Hurrell, *International Politics of the Environment* (Oxford: Clarendon Press, 1992), 1.

15 Oran Young, "Rights, Rules and Resources in World Affairs," in *Global Governance: Drawing Insights from the Environmental Experience*, ed. Oran Young (Cambridge, Mass.: MIT Press, 1997), 5–6; see also Oran Young, *Global Governance: Learning Lessons from the Environmental Experience* (Cambridge, Mass.: MIT Press, 1998); eds Peter Haas, Robert Keohane, and Marc Levy, *Institutions for the Earth: Sources of Effective Environmental Protection* (Cambridge, Mass.: MIT Press, 1993).

16 Peter Newell, *Climate for Change: Non-State Actors and the Global Politics of the Greenhouse* (Cambridge: Cambridge University Press, 2000), 23–4.

17 Matthew Paterson, *Global Warming, Global Politics* (London: Routledge, 1996); Chukwumerije Okereke and Harriet Bulkeley, "Conceptualizing Climate Change Governance Beyond the International Regime: A Review of Four Theoretical Approaches," *Tyndall Working Paper* 112 (2007), 6.

18 Susan Strange, "*Cave! Hic Dragones*: A Critique of Regime Analysis," *International Organization* 36 (1983): 488–90.

19 Paterson, *Global Warming, Global Politics*.

20 Marvin Soroos, "Global Climate Change and the Futility of the Kyoto Process," *Global Environmental Politics* 1, no. 2 (2001): 1–9.

21 Karen Litfin, *Ozone Discourses: Science and Politics in Global Environmental Cooperation* (New York: Columbia University Press, 1994).

22 Detlef Sprinz and Tapani Vaahtoranta, "The Interest-based Explanation of International Environmental Policy," *International Organization* 48 (1994): 77–105.

23 Okereke and Bulkeley, "Conceptualizing Climate Change Governance Beyond the International Regime: A Review of Four Theoretical Approaches," 6.

24 Harriet Bulkeley and Michele Betsill, *Cities and Climate Change: Urban Sustainability and Global Environmental Governance* (London: Routledge, 2003).

25 Newell, *Climate for Change: Non-State Actors and the Global Politics of the Greenhouse.*

26 Peter Haas, *Saving the Mediterranean: The Politics of International Environmental Cooperation* (New York: Columbia University Press, 1990), 349.

27 Paterson, *Global Warming, Global Politics.*

28 Paterson, *Global Warming, Global Politics*, 151.

29 Sheila Jasanoff and Brian Wynne, "Science and Decision Making," in *Human Choice and Climate Change I: The Societal Framework*, eds Steve Rayner and Elizabeth Malone (Columbus, Ohio: Battelle Press, 1998), 1–87.

30 Kathryn Harrison and Lisa McIntosh Sundstrom, eds, *Global Commons, Domestic Decisions: The Comparative Politics of Climate Change* (Cambridge Mass.: MIT, 2010).

31 Matthew Auer, "Who Participates in Global Environmental Governance? Partial Answers from International Relations Theory," *Policy Sciences* 33, no. 2 (2000): 155–80; Bulkeley and Betsill, *Cities and Climate Change: Urban Sustainability and Global Environmental Governance*; Harriet Bulkeley, "Reconfiguring Environmental Governance: Towards a Politics of Scales and Networks," *Political Geography* 24, no. 8 (2005): 875–902.

32 Newell, *Climate for Change: Non-State Actors and the Global Politics of the Greenhouse.*

33 Peter Newell, "The Political Economy of Global Environmental Governance," *Review of International Studies* 34 (July 2008): 507–29.

34 Newell and Paterson, "A Climate For Business," 679–704; Newell, "The Political Economy of Global Environmental Governance," 507–29.

35 Bulkeley, "Reconfiguring Environmental Governance: Towards a Politics of Scales and Networks," 875–902.

36 Ole Jacob Sending and Iver B. Neumann, "Governance to Governmentality: Analyzing NGOs, States, and Power," *International Studies Quarterly* 50, no. 3 (2006): 651–72.

37 John Allen, "Powerful City Networks: More than Connections, Less than Domination and Control," *Urban Studies*, 47, no. 13 (2010): 2895–911.

38 Thomas Risse, "Global Governance and Communicative Action," *Government and Opposition* 39, no. 2 (2004): 289.

39 James Rosenau, "Change, Complexity and Governance in a Globalizing Space," in *Debating Governance*, ed. Jon Pierre (Oxford: Oxford University Press, 2000), 172.

40 James Rosenau, "Governance, Order, and Change in World Politics," in *Governance Without Government: Order and Change in World Politics*, eds James Rosenau and Ernst Czempiel (Cambridge: Cambridge University Press, 1992), 6.

41 Klaus Dingwerth and Philipp Pattberg, "Global Governance as a Perspective on World Politics," *Global Governance* 12, no. 2 (2006): 185–203; Sverker Jagers and Johannes Stripple, "Climate Governance Beyond the State," *Global Governance* 9, no. 3 (2003): 385–99; Okereke and Bulkeley, "Conceptualizing

Climate Change Governance Beyond the International Regime: a Review of Four Theoretical Approaches"; Matthew Paterson, David Humphreys, and Lloyd Pettiford, "Conceptualizing Global Environmental Governance: From Interstate Regimes to Counter Hegemonic Struggles," *Global Environmental Politics* 3, no. 2 (2003): 1–8.

42 These are ideal types and there will of course be work which does not fit neatly into each category, while other authors may write from both perspectives. Note that we do not include here normative approaches to "global governance" associated with the drive by international organizations, nation-states and non-governmental bodies to promote "good" governance, though we acknowledge that such discourses share some liberal assumptions in common with academic approaches.

43 Sverker Jagers and Johannes Stripple, "Climate Governance Beyond the State," *Global Governance* 9, no. 3 (2003): 385.

44 Michele Betsill and Elisabeth Corell, eds, *NGO Diplomacy: The Influence of Nongovernmental Organizations in International Environmental Negotiations* (Cambridge, Mass.: MIT Press, 2008); Newell, *Climate for Change: Non-State Actors and the Global Politics of the Greenhouse*; Bas Arts, *The Political Influence of Global NGOs: Case Studies on the Climate and Biodiversity Conventions* (Utrecht, the Netherlands: International Books, 1998).

45 Lars H. Gulbrandsen and Steinar Andresen, "NGO Influence in the Implementation of the Kyoto Protocol: Compliance, Flexibility Mechanisms, and Sinks," *Global Environmental Politics* 4, no. 4 (2004): 56.

46 Betsill and Corell, *NGO Diplomacy: The Influence of Nongovernmental Organizations in International Environmental Negotiations*, 3.

47 Michele Betsill, "Transnational Actors in International Environmental Politics," in *Palgrave Advances in International Environmental Politics*, eds Michele M. Betsill, Kathryn Hochstetler, and Dimitris Stevis (Basingstoke, UK: Palgrave Macmillan, 2006), 191.

48 Dingwerth and Pattberg, "Global Governance as a Perspective on World Politics," 197.

49 Jagers and Stripple, "Climate Governance Beyond the State," 385.

50 Robert O. Keohane and David G. Victor, "The Regime Complex for Climate Change," *Discussion paper* 10–33 (Cambridge, Mass.: Harvard Project on International Climate Agreements, 2010), 1.

51 Fariborz Zelli, "The Fragmentation of the Global Climate Governance Architecture," *WIREs Climate Change* 2 (2011): 255–70.

52 Paul Wapner, *Environmental Activism and World Civic Politics* (Albany, N.Y.: State University of New York Press, 1996); Ronnie Lipschutz, "From Place to Planet: Local Knowledge and Global Environmental Governance," *Global Governance* 3, no. 1 (1997): 83–102.

53 Bulkeley and Betsill, *Cities and Climate Change: Urban Sustainability and Global Environmental Governance*; Henrik Selin and Stacy D. VanDeveer, "Canadian–US Environmental Cooperation: Climate Change Networks and Regional Action," *American Review of Canadian Studies* 35, no. 2 (2005): 353–78.

54 Karin Bäckstrand, "Accountability of Networked Climate Governance: The Rise of Transnational Climate Partnerships," *Global Environmental Politics* 8, no. 3 (2008): 74–102; Pattberg and Stripple, "Beyond the Public and Private Divide: Remapping Transnational Climate Governance in the 21st

Century"; Thorsten Benner, Wolfgang H. Reinicke, and Jan Martin Witte, "Multisectoral Networks in Global Governance: Towards a Pluralistic System of Accountability," *Government and Opposition* 39, no. 2 (2004): 191–210.

55 Benjamin Cashore, "Legitimacy and the Privatization of Environmental Governance: How Non-State Market-Driven Governance Systems Gain Rule-Making Authority," *Governance* 15, no. 4 (2004): 503–29; Jennifer Clapp, "The Privatization of Global Environmental Governance: ISO 14001 and the Developing World," *Global Governance* 4, no. 3 (1998); Klaus Dingwerth, "North–South Parity in Global Governance: The Affirmative Procedures of the Forest Stewardship Council," *Global Governance* 14, no. 1 (2008); Simone Pulver, "Importing Environmentalism: Explaining Petroleos Mexicanos' Proactive Climate Policy," *Studies in Comparative International Development* 42, no. 3/4 (2007): 233–55.

56 Peter Newell, Phillip Pattberg, and Heike Schroeder, "Multi-actor Governance and the Environment," *Annual Review of Environment and Resources* 37 (2012): 365–87.

57 Matthew Hoffman, *Climate Governance at the Crossroads: Experimenting with a Global Response after Kyoto* (Oxford: Oxford University Press, 2011); Harriet Bulkeley, Liliana Andonova, Michele M. Betsill, Daniel Compagnon, Thomas Hale, Peter Newell, Matthew Paterson, Charlie Rogers, and Stacy Vandever *Transnational Climate Change Governance* (Cambridge: Cambridge University Press, 2014).

58 Paul Wapner, "Governance in Global Civil Society," in *Global Governance: Drawing Insight from Environmental Experience*, ed. Oran Young (Cambridge, Mass.: MIT Press, 1997), 67.

59 Harriet Bulkeley and Heike Schroeder, "Beyond State/Non-State Divides: Global Cities and the Governing of Climate Change," *European Journal of International Relations* 18, no. 4 (2012): 743–66; Eva Lövbrand and Johannes Stripple, "Disrupting the Public–Private Distinction: Excavating the Government of Carbon Markets post-Copenhagen," *Environment and Planning C* 30 (2012): 658–74; Sending and Neumann, "Governance to Governmentality: Analyzing NGOs, States, and Power."

60 David Levy and Peter Newell, eds, *The Business of Global Environmental Governance* (Cambridge, Mass.: MIT Press, 2005); Matthew Paterson, *Understanding Global Environmental Politics: Domination, Accumulation and Resistance* (Houndmills, UK: Macmillan, 2000); Paterson, Humphreys, and Pettiford, "Conceptualizing Global Environmental Governance: From Interstate Regimes to Counter Hegemonic Struggles," 1–10; Julian Saurin, "Global Environmental Crisis as 'Disaster Triumphant': The Private Capture of Public Goods," *Environmental Politics* 10, no. 4 (2001): 80; Ulrich Brand and Markus Wissen, "Global Environmental Politics and the Imperial Mode of Living. Articulations of State–Capital Relations in the Multiple Crisis," *Globalizations* 9, no. 4 (2012): 547–60.

61 Bob Jessop, "Liberalism, Neoliberalism, and Urban Governance: A State-Theoretical Perspective," *Antipode* 34, no. 3 (2002): 463.

62 Chukwumerije Okereke, Harriet Bulkeley, and Heike Schroeder, "Conceptualizing Climate Governance Beyond the International Regime," *Global Environmental Politics* 9, no. 1 (2009): 58–78.

63 David Levy and Peter Newell, "Business Strategy and International Environmental Governance: Towards a Neo-Gramscian Synthesis," *Global Environmental Politics* 2, no. 4 (2002): 84–101; Levy and Newell, *The Business of Global Environmental Governance*.

64 Peter Newell, "The Political Economy of Global Environmental Governance," *Review of International Studies* 34 (2008): 507–29.

65 Michael Ekers and Alex Loftus, "The Power of Water: Developing Dialogues Between Foucault and Gramsci," *Environment and Planning D: Society and Space* 26, no. 4 (2008): 703.

66 Sending and Newmann, "Governance to Governmentality: Analyzing NGOs, States, and Power," 653.

67 See for example: Robyn Dowling, "Geographies of Identity: Climate Change, Governmentality and Activism," *Progress in Human Geography*, 34, no. 4 (2010): 488–95; Eva Lövbrand and Johannes Stripple, "Making Climate Change Governable: Accounting for Sinks, Credits and Personal Budgets," *Critical Policy Studies* 5, no. 2 (2011): 187–200; Heather Lovell, "Climate Change, Markets and Standards: The Case of Financial Accounting," *Economy and Society* 43, no. 2 (2014): 260–84; Angela Oels, "Rendering Climate Change Governable by Risk: From Probability to Contingency," *Geoforum* 45 (2013): 17–29; Johannes Stripple and Harriet Bulkeley, eds, *Governing the Climate: New Approaches to Rationality, Power and Politics* (New York: Cambridge University Press, 2014).

68 Sending and Newmann, "Governance to Governmentality: Analyzing NGOs, States, and Power," 657.

1

GOVERNING CLIMATE CHANGE

A brief history

Although we often assume that the high profile that climate change now enjoys means that it is a new political issue, in fact it has a much longer legacy. In this chapter, we provide a brief history of the politics of climate change. We analyze the key issues and conflicts in the international negotiations from the United Nations Framework Convention on Climate Change (UNFCCC) in 1992 through to the Kyoto Protocol in 1997 and up to the present state of negotiations towards an anticipated agreement in Paris in 2015. The discussion is organized around three features of climate governance which have characterized this period: the role of science and the scientific community in the governance of climate change, the evolving role of North–South politics, and finally the increasing marketization of climate governance. Before examining these key issues in turn, we provide a brief overview of how climate policy is made at the international level.

Making policy on climate change

Actors and institutions

The international negotiations on climate change are organized around a number of key actors, institutions, and decision making processes that it is necessary to understand to follow the discussion presented here. In terms of international organizations, three institutions are critical to the process of negotiating climate change policy. First, there is the secretariat of the UNFCCC, based in Bonn since 1996, which organizes and oversees the negotiations, prepares the necessary documentation, and is responsible for overseeing the reporting of emissions profiles and projects funded through the Kyoto Protocol. Guided by the parties to the Convention, it provides organizational support and technical expertise to the negotiations and institutions and facilitates the flow of authoritative information on the implementation of the Convention. It has a key and often underestimated role to play in shaping the outcomes of the negotiations.[1] It has an executive secretary who has the responsibility of trying to guide the negotiations towards a successful conclusion. Second, there is the Conference of the Parties (COP) to the UNFCCC which serves as the Meeting of the Parties to the Kyoto Protocol which meets annually to review progress on commitments contained in those treaties and to update them in the light of the latest scientific advice. This is the ultimate decision making body in the climate negotiations. Third, there are the Subsidiary Bodies for Implementation (SBI) and Scientific and Technological Advice (SBSTA) and the ad hoc working groups that take forward negotiations on specific issues which the COP ultimately has to approve. For example, there is at the moment an Ad Hoc Working Group on the Durban Platform for Enhanced Action. The links between these and other institutions which form the climate regime are illustrated in Figure 1.1.

In order to shape this process, governments often organize themselves into blocs and negotiating coalitions to enhance their influence and to advance common agendas. These key coalitions and negotiating blocs emerged early on in the negotiations, but have evolved significantly since then as the issues have changed and their levels of economic development dramatically altered.[2] At one end of the spectrum, the Organization of Petroleum Exporting Countries (OPEC) quickly emerged as the coalition of states most hostile to action on climate change. With revenues almost entirely dependent on the export of oil, that opposition was unsurprising. This bloc affected the pace and course of the negotiations, with calls for greater scientific certainty before action could take place, the formation of alliances with businesses opposed to action,[3] and the use of wrecking tactics such as the call for compensation for loss of oil revenue in response to the call from many low-lying developing countries for economic compensation for impacts suffered as a result of climate change.

At the other end of the spectrum, the Alliance of Small Island States (AOSIS), a coalition of island states most vulnerable to the effects of sea-level rise, has been the most strident of the negotiating coalitions in its demands for far-reaching and stringent emission reduction targets. In 1995, it proposed its own protocol to the agreement, mandating a 20 percent cut in 1990 emissions by 2005. The AOSIS group has worked closely with the London-based legal group Foundation for International Environmental Law and Development (FIELD) that provides legal advice on the negotiating text. Indeed, FIELD were attributed a key role in drafting the AOSIS protocol, suggesting the fragility of rigid distinctions about who exercises power and authority in the governance of climate change.[4]

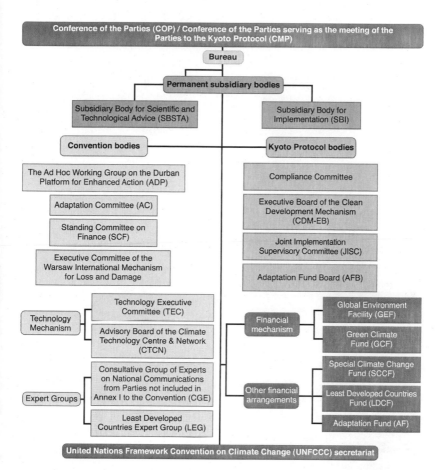

FIGURE 1.1 How the UN bodies dealing with climate change are related

Source: UNFCCC web site available online at http://unfccc.int/bodies/items/6241.php [accessed January 15, 2015].

In between these two polarities lay the coalition of the Group of 77 (G77) developing nations and China. This coalition emphasized the North's primary contribution to the problem of climate change and sought to deflect calls for the South to make commitments and to ensure that funds committed to achieving the Convention's goals were genuinely additional to existing money for aid. The G77, which, as we will see below, is now less cohesive, continues to provide a platform for shared concerns about climate change policy. The European Union, meanwhile, has been keen to see a stronger agreement, while the United States, particularly during the administrations of presidents George H.W. Bush and George W. Bush, was resolutely opposed to legally binding cuts in GHG. Japan has adopted a stance between these two positions, but has often been a reluctant leader because of high levels of industry pressure to not over-commit, and is now opposed to the idea of a second commitment period under the Kyoto Protocol. Both the United States and Japan were part of the JUSCANZ grouping (Japan, United States, Canada, Australia, and New Zealand) which argued for maximum flexibility in how countries were expected to meet their commitments in the negotiations towards the Kyoto Protocol. Now, along with Russia, many of these countries constitute the core group opposed to securing a second commitment period under the Kyoto Protocol. One notable development has been the growing power of so-called BRICS countries (Brazil, Russia, India, China, and South Africa) which became markedly apparent in the climate negotiations at the time of the Copenhagen summit in 2009 when President Obama and these leading, rapidly developing countries were the brokers of the Copenhagen Accord, and the European Union, previously thought of as a leader on climate change, was left out in the cold.

Alongside the formal negotiations organized in plenary sessions and working groups that meet in parallel to discuss specific issues, a bewildering array of non-governmental, business, and other organizations are registered to participate in the process. Though they do not have formal voting rights, they are allowed to make interventions and are often admitted onto government delegations where they have access to all the meetings taking place. In many ways, these actors are non-governmental "diplomats" that perform many of the same functions as state delegates: representing the interests of their constituencies, engaging in information exchange, negotiating, and providing policy advice.[5] Their participation, though growing, is nonetheless highly uneven. For example, although by the time of the Copenhagen summit in 2009, more than 1,000 organizations from 80 countries had obtained observer status, a closer look reveals the majority are based in Europe and North America. More than 210 organizations from the United States, for example, are registered as observers, alongside 100 groups from Britain and 92 from Canada. Meanwhile, no developing country, except for Brazil, China, and India, managed to bring more than ten observer organizations to the table.[6]

We can see, therefore, that the process of making climate policy involves international organizations and institutional structures established for this purpose, coalitions and blocs of state actors, and a range of non-state actors who have sought to influence the process of negotiation in a variety of ways. Before turning to discuss particular aspects of this process in detail, we first consider the main policy milestones that have shaped the current state of international climate policy.

Climate change policy milestones

The governance of climate change as a global political issue has progressed from being a cause for concern among a growing number of scientists to gaining recognition as an issue deserving of a collective global effort orchestrated by the United Nations (UN) (Box 1.1). Over time, there has been a deepening of cooperation and firming up of obligations to act; this is a process common to many international negotiations on the environment where a general agreement identifies the need for action and a subsequent protocol contains concrete legally binding emission reduction commitments. What is also notable, a theme to which we return below, is the increasing use of market or flexible mechanisms to achieve emission reductions.

BOX 1.1 THE GLOBAL GOVERNANCE OF CLIMATE CHANGE: A SHORT CHRONOLOGY

1988   World Conference on the Changing Atmosphere: politicians and scientists conclude that "humanity is conducting an unintended, uncontrolled, globally pervasive experiment whose ultimate consequences could be second only to nuclear war." The conference recommends reducing CO_2 emissions by 20 percent by 2005.

1990   The IPCC publishes its *First Assessment Report.*

1991   The Intergovernmental Negotiating Committee is set up to oversee negotiations towards an international agreement

1992   In Rio de Janeiro 154 countries sign the UNFCCC at the United Nations Conference on Environment and Development. The aim is to stabilize emissions at 1990 levels by the year 2000 as part of an overall goal to stabilize GHG "concentrations in the atmosphere at a level that would prevent dangerous interference with the climate system."[a]

1994   The UNFCCC enters into force on March 21.

1995   The first COP agrees in Berlin that binding commitments by industrialized countries are required to reduce emissions.

1995   The IPCC publishes its *Second Assessment Report,* which suggests that "The balance of evidence suggests a discernible human influence on global climate."[b]

1996   The second COP in Geneva sees the United States agree to legally binding targets to reduce emissions as long as emissions trading is included in an agreement.

1997   More than 150 countries sign the Kyoto Protocol which binds 38 industrialized (Annex 1) countries to reduce GHG emissions by an average of 5.2 percent below 1990 levels during the period 2008–12.

2000   The negotiations at the sixth COP in The Hague collapse amid disagreements, principally between the United States and Europe, about the use of the Kyoto Protocol's flexibility mechanisms.

2001   President George W. Bush announces that the US is to withdraw from the Kyoto Protocol.

2001	In Marrakesh the final elements of the Kyoto Protocol are worked out, particularly the rules and procedures by which the flexible mechanisms will operate.
2004	The Buenos Aires Programme of Work on Adaptation and Response Measures is agreed at COP 10.
2005	On February 16, the Kyoto Protocol becomes law after Russian ratification pushes the emissions of ratified Annex 1 countries over the 55 percent mark.[*]
2005	The first Meeting of the Parties to the Kyoto Protocol takes place in Montreal at COP 11.
2006	At the Second Meeting of the Parties (COP 12), the Nairobi Work Programme on Adaptation and the Nairobi Framework on Capacity-Building for the CDM are agreed.
2007	The IPCC publishes its *Fourth Assessment Report*.
2007	At COP 13 the Bali Action Plan is agreed, which calls for a long-term goal for emission reductions; measurable, reportable, verifiable mitigation commitments including nationally appropriate mitigation actions by LDCs; enhanced adaptation, action on technology development and transfer, and financial resources and investment to support the above.
2009	The COP 15 takes place in Copenhagen amid pressure to "seal the deal" on a new legally binding agreement. Instead, a small group of countries negotiated the Copenhagen Accord, which other parties would only "note" the existence of. Industrialized nations committed to provide developing nations with US$30 billion of "new and additional" fast-track funding between 2010 and 2012, as well as US$100 billion per year by 2020 to be channelled through a Green Climate Fund.
2010	COP 16 agrees the "Cancún agreements" which seek to keep the negotiations on track in the areas of adaptation, forests, climate finance, technology transfer, and capacity building in the wake of the fiasco at Copenhagen.
2011	In Durban at COP17, governments commit to adopt a universal legal agreement on climate change as soon as possible, but not later than 2015, to come into effect in 2020. A new group called the Ad Hoc Working Group on the Durban Platform for Enhanced Action takes this forward.
2014	The IPCC *Fifth Assessment Report* is published.[c] It concludes that "Human influence on the climate system is clear, and recent anthropogenic emissions of greenhouse gases are the highest in history. Recent climate changes have had widespread impacts on human and natural systems . . . Their effects, together with those of other anthropogenic drivers, have been detected throughout the climate system and are *extremely likely* to have been the dominant cause of the observed warming since the mid-20th century."
2014	COP20 meets in Lima under pressure to quicken the pace of progress towards a new global deal to be completed and signed in Paris at the end of 2015.

Sources:
  [1] Article 2 of the UNFCCC (1992) available at http://unfccc.int/essential_background/convention/items/6036.php [accessed January 15, 2015].
  [2] IPCC, *Second Assessment Report* (Cambridge: Cambridge University Press, 1995).
  [3] IPCC *Fifth Assessment Report* available at http://www.ipcc.ch/ [accessed January 15, 2015].

* Note: Article 25 of the Kyoto Protocol specifies that it enters into force "on the ninetieth day after the date on which not less than 55 Parties to the Convention, incorporating Parties included in Annex I which accounted in total for at least 55% of the total carbon dioxide emissions for 1990 of the Annex I countries, have deposited their instruments of ratification, acceptance, approval or accession." The "55 parties clause" was reached on May 23, 2002 when Iceland ratified the Protocol. The ratification by Russia on November 18, 2004 satisfied the "55%" clause and brought the treaty into force, effective February 16, 2005.

The UNFCCC was agreed at the United Nations Conference on Environment and Development (UNCED) summit in Rio in 1992. As the first major milestone in the history of climate diplomacy, the UNFCCC provided a framework for global action on the issue. It sought to emulate the apparent success of the ozone regime, which first produced the Vienna Convention, establishing the nature of the problem and the basis for action on it, and subsequently the Montreal Protocol, which agreed a phase-out of the most damaging ozone-depleting chemicals. Given the sharp differences of opinion described above, and the relative lack of momentum behind the issue at the time, the fact the UNFCCC was agreed at all can be considered a considerable achievement. The agreement set the goal of "avoiding dangerous interference in the climate system," defined as aiming to stabilize concentrations of GHG in the atmosphere, and listed some of policies and measures that countries might adopt to achieve that end. Acknowledging the vast differences in contributions to the problem, the Convention established the principle of "common but differentiated responsibility"[7] and recognized that developing countries were not yet in a position to assume their own obligations. Efforts they could make towards tackling the issue were made dependent on the receipt of aid and technology transfer from Northern countries that were meant to be "additional" to existing aid budgets.

Attention then turned to how to realize the general nature of the commitments contained in the UNFCCC. With scientific assessments of the severity of climate change becoming increasingly common, and growing awareness of the inadequacy of existing policy responses, momentum built for a follow-up to the Convention.[8] The 1995 Berlin Mandate at the first COP sought to promote Quantifiable Emissions Limitations and Reduction Obligations (QELROs) and negotiations thus began towards a Protocol which would set legally binding targets to reduce GHG emissions. The Kyoto Protocol, concluded in 1997, was the outcome of this. Signed by more than 150 countries, it binds 38 industrialized (Annex 1) countries to reduce GHG emissions by an average of 5.2 percent below 1990 levels during the period 2008–12 (see Box 1.2). It fixes differentiated targets for industrialized countries while setting in train a process to further elaborate joint implementation schemes, to set up an emissions trading scheme (ETS), and to create a Clean Development Mechanism (CDM). We discuss these further below.

> **BOX 1.2 THE KYOTO PROTOCOL IN BRIEF**
>
> Commitments
>
> - Industrialized countries were required to reduce their collective emissions of GHG by an average of 5.2 percent below 1990 levels in the commitment period 2008–12.
> - The US was to reduce its emissions by an average of 7 percent, Japan by an average of 6 percent, and the EU by an average of 8 percent. Other industrialized countries were permitted small increases, while others were obliged only to freeze their emissions.
> - Developed countries were obliged to provide:
>   - "new and additional financial resources to meet the agreed full costs incurred by developing country Parties in advancing the implementation of existing commitments"
>   - "such financial resources, including transfer of technology, needed by the developing country parties to meet the agreed and full incremental costs of advancing the implementation of existing commitments" and
>   - "financial resources for the implementation of Article 10, through bilateral, regional and other multilateral channels" of which developing country parties can avail themselves.
>
> Instruments
>
> - Clean Development Mechanism—The aim of this body is to assist developing countries in achieving sustainable development and

at the same time to help developed countries "in achieving compliance with their quantified emission limitation and reduction commitments" (Article 12). In effect its purpose is to authorize projects funded by developed states wanting to accrue credits for emission reductions achieved overseas. Certified Emissions Reduction credits are distributed by the CDM Executive Board to projects generating "additional" emissions reductions. In addition, a tax applied to transactions in the CDM generates revenue for the Adaptation Fund.

- Joint Implementation/Actions Implemented Jointly—Defined in Article 6 of the Kyoto Protocol, this allows a country with an emission reduction or limitation commitment under the Kyoto Protocol to earn emission reduction units (ERUs) from an emission-reduction or emission-removal project in another Annex B (more industrialized country) Party.
- Emissions Trading (Article 17).
- Implementation will be via national reports overseen by teams of experts nominated by the Parties.

Note: Parties were expected to have demonstrated progress in reaching the Kyoto target by the year 2005. Cuts in the three important gases (CO_2, NH_4, and NO_2) will be calculated against a base year of 1990, and cuts in the long-lived industrial gases (hydrofluorocarbons, perfluorocarbons and sulfur hexafluoride) can be measured against a base year of either 1990 or 1995.

The process for finalizing the rules and operational details of the Protocol was agreed at COP 4 in 1998 as part of the Buenos Aires Plan of Action. In November 2000, parties met in The Hague at COP 6 to try to complete these negotiations, but failed to do so amid a growing rift between, in particular, the European Union and the United States.[9] Having been party to the negotiations and after lobbying hard for the inclusion of market-based mechanisms which would allow industrialized countries maximum flexibility, in 2001 the United States walked away from the Kyoto Protocol. We will see below that part of the United States' refusal to ratify Kyoto was because its economic competitors in the developing world were not required to reduce their emissions. Without the involvement of the United States, many assumed the inevitable demise of the Kyoto Protocol. If the largest contributor to the problem and most powerful economy in the world was not on board, what incentive was there for others to sign up? In fact, the absence of the United States served to galvanize the European Union and the G77 + China into further action, and with the Russian ratification of the Kyoto Protocol in 2005 it entered into force.

Subsequent negotiations have focused on detailed issues concerning the implementation and enforcement of Kyoto and, increasingly, what might come in its place. At the COP 7, the Marrakesh Accords were agreed, which established the rules and procedures for the operation of the flexible mechanisms including the CDM, as well as details on reporting and methodologies. Importantly, they also established three new funds: the Least Developed Countries Fund, the Special Climate Change Fund, and the Adaptation Fund. This work was continued through to the Buenos Aires Programme of Work on Adaptation and Response Measures agreed at COP 10 in 2004. This was followed at COP 11 in Montreal with the creation of the Ad Hoc Working Group on Further Commitments for Annex 1 parties under the Kyoto Protocol. At COP 12 in Nairobi, dubbed the "Africa COP," there was significant discussion about financing issues and how to increase the number of CDM projects being hosted by the poorest regions of the world, most notably sub-Saharan Africa. The meeting produced the Nairobi Work Programme on Adaptation and the Nairobi Framework on Capacity-Building for the CDM.[10] The Bali Action Plan, agreed a year later at COP 13, set the path for negotiations towards Copenhagen, calling for a long-term goal for emission reductions; measurable, reportable, verifiable mitigation commitments, including nationally appropriate mitigation actions by Least Developed Countries (LDCs); as well as enhanced adaptation, action on technology development and transfer, and financial resources and investment to support the above.[11] Unfortunately, the 2009 COP 15 meeting in Copenhagen failed to agree a new legally binding agreement despite intense pressure to "seal the deal." A "Copenhagen Accord" was produced by a small number of powerful countries including China, India, Brazil, and South Africa—reflecting the growing economic and political power of those countries, as well as their own rising contribution to the problem of climate change. This established the aim of limiting warming to 2°C compared with preindustrial levels, but provided no measures to achieve this. Annex 1 (richer country) Parties committed to implement individually or jointly the quantified economy-wide emissions targets for 2020 while non-Annex 1 Parties to the Convention agreed to implement mitigation actions subject to international measurement, reporting, and verification in accordance with guidelines adopted by the Conference of the Parties. The failure of the meeting to advance progress and the breakdown in trust that occurred left the negotiations in a state of disarray.

This was, at least in part, rectified by the Cancún meeting in 2010, which agreed a series of decisions on key areas of the Bali Action Plan, on issues such as finance—most notably the creation of the Green Climate Fund—as well as technology cooperation and adaptation. In Durban in 2011, governments decided to adopt a universal legal agreement on climate change as soon as possible, but not later than 2015, to come into effect in 2020 under the auspices of the Ad Hoc Working Group on the Durban Platform for Enhanced Action (ADP). States are divided between those 38 industrialized countries that agreed on a second commitment period of the Kyoto Protocol from January 1, 2013, and the powerful countries that continue to be opposed to a second commitment period (including the United States, Japan, and Canada) who prefer a universal platform including all countries. By 2013, 42 developed countries had submitted economy-wide GHG emission reduction pledges, 16 developing countries had submitted multisector expected emission reductions, and in addition, 39 other developing countries had submitted pledges related to sectoral goals.[12] Yet, the United Nations Environment Programme (UNEP) calculates that existing pledges provide only 60 percent of the GHG reductions needed to cap warming at 2°C.[13] The world is thus on track towards a 4°C temperature rise,[14] should the currently inadequate level of ambition remain. This leaves significant work to be done at the critical Paris summit in 2015 when a new global agreement is expected to be concluded.

However, after almost three years of these ADP negotiations, the outcome of the latest round of these negotiations is still far from agreeing the key elements of a global agreement to be finalized in 2015. If the new agreement is to include legally binding elements in the form of a protocol or similar instrument, under the rules of procedure of the UNFCCC, these legally binding elements would have to be submitted for consideration six months prior to COP 21 in Paris, which would be by the end of May 2015. Time to have an ambitious new global deal in place within this time frame is clearly running out.

Climate becomes political: science and climate governance

As we have seen above, the process of making climate policy has been shaped by a complex mix of institutions and actors. One of the key issues has been the interface between science and policy which provided the first impetus for international agreement and continues to be central to global climate politics.

The greenhouse effect—in which particular atmospheric gases, so-called greenhouse gases, act to increase the amount of energy retained in the Earth's atmosphere—was discovered by Joseph Fourier in 1824. Other scientists such as the physicist John Tyndall helped to further identify the relative radiative forcing values of the different GHG before the greenhouse effect was first investigated quantitatively by Svante Arrhenius in 1896. The basic science behind the greenhouse effect is graphically portrayed in Figure 1.2. This is a naturally occurring phenomenon. However, by increasing the proportion of GHG in the atmosphere, human activities can exacerbate this effect leading to higher globally average temperatures and changes in the climate. Despite the early discoveries noted above, it was not until the late 1970s, according to climate scientist Bert Bolin, that this "possibility of human-induced change of climate first caught the attention of politicians."[15] During the early 1980s, the first international assessment

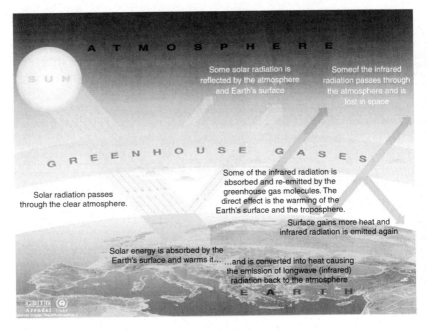

FIGURE 1.2 The greenhouse effect and climate change

Source: Okanagan University College in Canada, Department of Geography, University of Oxford, School of Geography; United States Environmental Protection Agency (EPA), Washington; Climate Change 1995, The science of climate change, constitution of working group 1 to the second assessment report of the intergovernmental panel on climate change, UNEP and WMO, Cambridge University Press, 1996.

of climate change was convened, supported by the International Council of Scientific Unions (ICSU) and the World Meteorological Organization (WMO), which concluded with the Villach conference in 1985 and an appeal to the international community to address the issue seriously.

The IPCC was then established in 1988 to provide expert input into the climate negotiations but to be directed in its mandate by governmental representatives. It was formed by WMO and UNEP. The IPCC is an expert body made up of the world's leading climate scientists in areas such as oceanography, climatology, meteorology, and economics to produce reports, subject to widespread peer review, on the latest scientific understanding of climate change. Successive reports by the body issued in 1990, 1995, 2001, 2007, and 2014 have provided a substantive and consolidated knowledge base about three dimensions of the climate change problem: (i) the science and the basic causal mechanisms, (ii) impacts, and (iii) response strategies: economic, technical, and policy implications. Working groups have been created to provide policymakers with the latest research in each of these areas.

Though charged with the responsibility of providing independent and objective advice on the latest scientific understanding of all aspects of the problem of climate change, its work has been heavily politicized from the very outset. Science has been a key battleground in the debate about climate change: the severity of the threat, the nature of the causal mechanisms and probable impacts, and the economic costs associated with taking action. Scientific knowledge is used by all actors in climate governance to advance and defend their position, and to confer legitimacy upon it. It is the perception of science as objective and above politics that makes it attractive to actors who believe it provides them with a trump card over the claims of others. However, decisions about whose knowledge counts, who wields authority, and how knowledge is presented and framed are deeply political processes that imply the exercise of power. As Foucault argues:

> we should admit . . . that power and knowledge directly imply one another; that there is no power relation without the correlative constitution of a field of knowledge, nor any knowledge that does not at the same time presuppose and constitute power relations.[16]

It is unsurprising that the process of accumulating and presenting scientific evidence and advice about the climate change issue has been so political. There is a lot at stake. We see this with the production of policymakers' summaries of the latest IPCC reports, the most widely read part of the report. Business, NGOs, and government representatives are allowed to participate in the drafting of these summaries and actively seek to shape their content to reflect their views of the severity of climate change, highlighting uncertainties in the case of those opposed to action or drawing attention to warnings about the potential for dramatic feed-back effects by those wanting more stringent near-term action. As former IPCC chairman Bert Bolin reflects:

> the Summary for Policy-makers is approved in a plenary session of the respective working groups . . . [these] become the occasions when the scientists engaged by the IPCC are confronted with political views and even attempts to clothe special interests in scientific terms.[17]

Recognizing the interwoven nature of power and knowledge challenges the assumption that science interacts with policy in a fairly linear way where governments and international institutions are dependent on experts—sometimes labeled epistemic communities—to advise them on political actions in conditions of uncertainty.[18] In practice, the worlds of science and politics overlap. One of the key roles of scientists is to act as "knowledge brokers,"[19] translators of abstract scientific findings into policy messages, intermediaries between lab and law. The fact that scientists are also often dependent on government money for their research has led some to claim that the alleged urgency of the threat posed by climate change has been deliberately exaggerated by a scientific community keen to attract research funding for further work in the area.[20] Once established in a well-resourced and high-profile policy network, so this argument goes, scientists develop their own self-interests in maintaining that position and securing funding for their work. Another source of potent criticism has been that important uncertainties in the science and modeling have been downplayed or ignored altogether. This has been the line of attack of a relatively small but vocal group of so-called climate skeptics who either doubt that global warming results from anthropogenic influences or suggest that the scale of that influence has been over-estimated.[21] The so-called "climate-gate" scandal involving the illegal accessing and release of hundreds of email communications from the accounts of researchers at the University of East Anglia's prestigious Climate Research Unit appeared to provide fodder for these claims, though subsequent hearings which acquitted the climate scientists of any wrong-doing received far less public exposure than the damaging claims made at the time of the release of the emails.[22] Given the contentious ground which the IPCC occupies it is also unsurprising that senior appointments within the IPCC have also been a source of controversy.

For example, the US government successfully vetoed the reappointment of Bob Watson as head of the IPCC amid claims he was pursuing a personal agenda which was interpreted at the time as being too outspoken an advocate of climate action.[23]

One of the key issues here is not only that politics get played out through science, but the way science is used politically. While the UNFCCC refers to the prevention of "dangerous anthropogenic interference in the climate system"[24] as the overall goal of the agreement, defining what counts as "dangerous" is a political act, a judgment about risk: how much risk we, as a society, are willing to take and who bears the consequences. A key battleground in the negotiations towards the UNFCCC was whether sufficient scientific consensus existed to warrant global collective action. Those against more strident forms of action demanded more science as if that was the key obstacle to action. As the NGO newsletter *ECO* declared at the Geneva climate meeting back in 1990, "all the computer models in the world will not make a Swiss Franc of difference to governments who simply want to sell all the oil the world can be persuaded to buy."[25] Part of the reason the interface between science and policy is so contested is because of the political significance of recommendations that are made for identifying and allocating responsibility. This has been a highly contested issue between developed and developing countries and it is to this issue that we now turn.

The poverty of climate governance: North–South politics

The second dimension of climate governance which cuts across this history of climate diplomacy is the importance of North–South politics. Climate change in many ways highlights more starkly the North–South divisions which characterize other global environmental threats such as ozone depletion and biodiversity.[26] Early battles about the need to differentiate between the "survival" emissions of the South and the "luxury" emissions of the North[27] have been compounded by claims of carbon colonialism and climate injustice as we will see in Chapter 2. Underpinning this conflict is the fact that, while climate change has been largely caused by the wealthy industrialized parts of the world, it is the least developed parts of the world that will suffer its worst consequences. This makes climate change first and foremost an issue of social justice and equity.

Early discussions of the climate change issue demonstrated a clear polarity of positions between developed countries and developing countries with the latter arguing that the former, as leading contributors to the problem, were duty bound to accept responsibility and take action. The language in the UNFCCC embodies this notion of "common but differentiated responsibility,"[28] the idea that everybody has a responsibility to act but some have more responsibility than others. Insofar as developing (or non-Annex 1) countries have responsibilities under the convention, these are conditional on the receipt of aid and technology transfer from more developed countries. Aid and technology transfer provide what economists would refer to as side-payments: inducements to cooperate in tackling a problem to which, historically speaking, they have contributed very little.

Debate has focused on the governance of aid and technology transfer; which institution will oversee these and on whose terms. While developed countries were keen to see the Global Environment Facility (GEF) play a key role, the institution's close association with the World Bank was a source of concern for many developing countries that were distrustful of the organization.[29] Many developing countries also expressed reservations about the levels and types of aid that would be forthcoming. They sought forms of financial assistance that were "additional" to existing aid budgets and not drawn from budget lines targeted for other development priorities. Concerns by developing countries in particular continue to be expressed about the World Bank's role as interim trustee of the Green Climate Fund, the key body called for under the Copenhagen Accord to distribute the US$100 billion that countries have committed to providing for climate mitigation and adaptation annually by 2020.

The presentation of a united front by the G77 on these key issues always disguised a spectrum of diverse national and regional differences. Over time, however, divisions among developing countries have become more apparent and more clearly defined. Increasing emphasis in the global debate about the use of flexible market mechanisms endorsed by the Kyoto Protocol forced developing countries to assess how they might engage with and benefit from such mechanisms. Interest in the role of forests as carbon sinks for which credits might be earned and finance provided to developing countries, has drawn bio-diverse countries, particularly many Latin American countries, further into the realm of joint actions.[30] At the same time, the newly industrializing power houses of China, India, Brazil, Malaysia, Mexico, and South Korea now make their own significant contribution to the problem, raising further questions about how the principle of "common but differentiated responsibilities" should be put into practice.

In this context, there is an ongoing debate about whether, and if so, in what form, developing countries should take on their own emission reduction commitments, an issue which came to a head at the time of the Copenhagen summit. There is a perception among some developed countries that rapidly industrializing competitors will be able to free-ride on the sacrifices made by Annex 1 parties. The related concern is that industries will uproot and relocate to areas of the world not covered by the provisions of the Kyoto Protocol, resulting in "carbon leakage."[31] Increasing recognition of this new geography of responsibility prompted demands from leading polluters—such as the United States and Australia—to draw their competitors into a global regime of regulation and controls on GHG. Most dramatically, at the time of the Kyoto negotiations in 1997, Senator Chuck Hagel drafted the Byrd–Hagel resolution (Senate Resolution 98) which made US acceptance of the terms of the Kyoto Protocol conditional on agreement from leading developing countries to reduce their own emissions. Given the sensitivity about the issue of legally binding emission reduction obligations for developing countries, this strategy was aimed at causing maximum divisions, stalling progress, and most importantly tying the hands of US negotiators by showing that the senate would not ratify any deal which did not contain developing country commitments. Indeed, it was this issue in part that led the United States, under George W. Bush, to withdraw from the Kyoto Protocol in 2001.

Since that time, many developing countries have indeed adopted voluntary obligations to reduce their emissions or reduce the carbon intensity of their growth trajectories, though in many cases continuing to resist calls for binding reduction commitments. This is the case for China, India, and South Africa, with, for example, the South African government committing itself at the Copenhagen summit in 2009 to reduce its GHG emissions by 34 percent by 2020 and 44 percent by 2025. Acknowledgement of the shifting geography of responsibility for emissions underpins moves to abandon the Kyoto Protocol "fire-wall" between Annex 1 (more industrialized) and non-Annex 1 (less industrialized) countries and include these countries in a new round of commitments under the auspices of the UNFCCC.

Besides the issue of responsibility, there is also a clear North–South dimension in terms of vulnerability to the effects of climate change (particularly sea-level rise and changes to agricultural systems). In terms of impacts of climate change, developing countries are in a weaker position to protect themselves from the adverse effects of climate change. Sea defenses and other means available to wealthier nations to ensure that land is not flooded and that population displacement is not necessary are not affordable to many developing countries. Their reliance on agricultural production on many low-lying areas that are especially prone to flooding from sea-level rise, makes them particularly vulnerable to the effects of climate change. This is an issue we return to in Chapter 2.

These uneven patterns of responsibility for emissions of GHG and vulnerability to the effects of climate change have profoundly affected efforts to secure global agreements on climate change. The broader historical and contemporary features of the unequal relationship between the developed and developing world run through virtually all aspects of climate change governance.[32] Scientists from developing countries are poorly represented in the expert bodies that provide the knowledge base for policy. Poorer groups within these countries are disproportionately vulnerable to the effects of climate change, even if they contribute little to the problem. In many cases, governments of developing countries lack the capacity to attend, let alone shape and influence, negotiating processes that are heavily dominated by developed countries with the resources to attend all meetings and the legal and scientific capacity to shape developments according to their preferences. The politics of North–South relations have therefore both explicitly and implicitly shaped the history of international climate change policy, with profound implications for how the issue is addressed. We return to this debate in Chapter 2.

The marketization of climate governance

The third notable feature of climate governance which cuts across this history is the increasing emphasis on market-based solutions.[33] Often referred to as "flexibility mechanisms," the right of countries to meet their obligations through funding emission reductions elsewhere through the joint implementation of projects or through the buying and selling of permits has been asserted forcefully by the world's most powerful country, the United States. As we can see in Box 1.2, the Kyoto Protocol that was agreed in December 1997 embodied a commitment to constructing such flexible mechanisms. The CDM market took off rapidly. The global value of primary offset transactions grew to US$7.2 billion in 2008, more than a ten-fold growth from 2004, largely due to the CDM. Under the CDM, certified emissions reductions (CERs) amounting to more than 1.8 billion tons of carbon dioxide equivalent(CO_2e) were produced in the first commitment period of the Kyoto Protocol (2008–12) and over the period 2001 to 2012, the CDM is claimed to have spurred US$215 billion in investment.[34]

The support for market-based approaches as the preferred means of climate governance reflects a number of factors. The endorsement of emissions trading in particular built on the alleged effectiveness of other flexible and voluntary approaches, most notably the United States' sulfur dioxide trading scheme. Such approaches reflect the primacy of efficiency as the guiding policy principle of climate change governance. In this vein, advocates have argued that it makes no difference where in the world a ton of GHG is reduced and therefore it makes sense to create mechanisms which allow countries to pay for reductions where it is most cost-effective to do so. In terms of domestic politics, such mechanisms make emission reductions easier to sell to electorates wary of burdening domestic industry with additional obligations and therefore creates scope to raise the level of ambition. Such tools were also seen as a valuable way of bridging some of the North–South conflicts discussed above. They could imply resource transfers to developing countries, potentially on a significant scale. Indeed, according to the World Bank, revenues from the CDM constitute the largest source of mitigation finance to developing countries to date.[35] And because emissions are being reduced in these countries, they draw them further into the climate regime, pacifying concerns about them free-riding on the sacrifices made by more industrialized countries.

That the world of climate governance has become a laboratory for experiments in market-based approaches to regulation is unsurprising, given that climate politics have risen to prominence during an era of heightened neo-liberalism.[36] This broader political context is important in explaining why some solutions are seen as valid, legitimate, and plausible, and others are not. It helps us to understand why, for example, command and control state-led regulatory approaches are out of favor, or why, in a context of globalization and the mobility of capital, it becomes more important than ever to address potential carbon leakage. The emphasis in contemporary neo-liberalism on the creation of (carbon) markets, the allocation of property rights (in this case through allocating permits), the political preference for voluntary partnership-based approaches and self-regulation by industry is clearly apparent in all aspects of contemporary climate governance, as we will see in Chapter 5. The irony, of course, was that having insisted on the inclusion of market-based mechanisms, the United States then refused to ratify the Kyoto Protocol. The European Union, meanwhile, which had initially been hostile to the idea of emissions trading, went on to develop the most advanced emission trading scheme of its kind, the EU Emissions Trading Scheme.[37]

Despite the prevalence of the idea that markets deliver outcomes more efficiently and effectively than governments, each of the market-based mechanisms mentioned here relies on institutional backing. Governments have to decide who can participate in carbon markets (which sectors and actors) and set limits on the number of permits that are to be traded to create the necessary scarcity to incentivize emission reductions. Markets, in other words, have to be made and then governed. The 2001 Marrakesh Accords explicitly aimed to agree to rules, procedures, and modalities for the operation of the CDM for example (Chapter 2). Furthermore, in order to guarantee the worth of the CER units that are allocated, a range of governance actors have to be enrolled to verify baselines and methodologies to demonstrate beyond doubt that emissions are "additional" (that they would not otherwise have been achieved by other means). Project developers help set up projects and a CDM Executive Board approves methodologies and projects. Harnessing the market to the goal of climate protection is one thing, but it does not do away with the need for inputs from traditional actors in climate governance such as states, and international institutions.

Indeed, these actors have been called upon repeatedly to bail-out carbon markets encountering recurrent crises in the same way they have had to bail out financial markets in the wake of the global economic crisis which began in 2008. We are currently at a key juncture in the debate about the role of carbon markets in responses to climate change. On the one hand, the low price of carbon and the declining interest on the part of financial capital, thought to be one of the main beneficiaries of carbon trading, and repeated scandals which have engulfed the CDM and the EU Emissions Trading Scheme (ETS), have led to claims of their imminent demise.[38] On the other hand, carbon markets, judged by their on-going proliferation, are flourishing. At the UN level, the negotiations are focused on the construction of new market mechanisms. Governments in Annex 1 countries continue to construct mechanisms and streams of finance to support the growth and interlinkage of carbon markets (such as the UK government's Carbon Market Finance Initiative). And at a regional and national level, a swathe of new carbon markets and emission trading schemes are coming online in countries like China, South Korea, Vietnam, Thailand, Australia, and Mexico. Despite their apparent failings, therefore, a strong level of ideological, material, and institutional commitment to carbon markets on the part of states and corporations as the preferred solution to climate change, means that the marketization of climate governance looks set to continue.

Governance issues and challenges

This chapter draws our attention to a number of general features of climate governance. First, though climate change is often talked about as a global governance challenge, those countries whose actions directly determine the shape and effectiveness of the regime are relatively few in number. Deal-brokering, unsurprisingly, tends to focus on those actors. Traditionally, these have been the United States, the European Union, and Japan. The rising economic power of countries like China, India, Brazil, and South

Africa means that they also are increasingly privy to head-to-head closed meetings in which negotiators attempt to establish the basic contours of agreement within which cooperation might be possible, as the Copenhagen summit made strikingly clear. The key deal-brokers in climate governance have changed in a way which reflects shifts in economic power in the global economy. The scope and nature of the negotiations mirrors broader geo-political and economic shifts in another way too: the support for market mechanisms as the preferred way of governing climate change in spite of their poor track record to date.[39] Climate governance cannot be understood as separate from the ideology, institutions, and material interests that predominate within the wider global economy which affect the nature of climate politics and, if it is to be effective, climate governance needs to engage with and change them.

Second, although traditional approaches to understanding global environmental politics focus on bargaining between nation-states at the international level, they often neglect the importance of domestic politics. Various researchers have revealed the dynamic relationship whereby what happens in the domestic arenas of global powers carries global repercussions, just as what is agreed in global forums reconfigures domestic politics.[40] We have seen in this chapter, particularly in relation to the role of the United States, how global arenas are also a site of domestic politics and domestic politics get played out globally. Analytical distinctions which attempt to neatly separate the two are poorly served by the reality of networks, coalitions, and messy politics that cut across these levels of analysis. Importantly, as we will see in Chapter 2, the effectiveness of traditional climate governance in the form of national regulation and the forms of public international law described here, and the spaces and places where it is said to take place (within states and international institutions), is contingent on the ability and willingness of these governance actors and processes to engage with and seek to transform the everyday practices of climate governance that go by the names of energy policy, development policy, trade, industry, and agricultural policy. These are blind-spots or areas of active neglect in the governance of climate change whose future path will determine whether our collective responses to climate change are up to the challenge.

Third, non-state actors are central to the governance of climate change. Even in the traditionally speaking, relatively closed world of interstate diplomacy, non-state actors are on delegations, in the conference rooms, talking to the media and protesting outside. The neat distinctions that underpin the official roles and status ascribed to non-state actors describe poorly the reality of actors and individuals that move in and out of these categories, constructing and participating in coalitions and network formations that bypass traditional "levels of analysis," and producing hybrid forms of climate governance in their wake.[41] Whether it is the scientific community, business lobbies, or environmental groups, each of these actors plays a role and draws on assets that go beyond what governments and international institutions, the traditional agents on climate politics, can deliver alone.[42] As carbon markets assume increasing importance in the delivery of emission reductions, business actors in particular assume a more important role than ever before. NGOs are increasingly enrolled as project developers, monitors, and watchdogs. Indeed with so many governance sites beyond the international regime that form part of the climate change "regime complex,"[43] the UN faces a struggle to retain relevance and some non-state actors have moved their sights elsewhere. While there are many competing explanations about why the international climate change regime takes the form it does, some of which we discuss in the Introduction (knowledge-based, interest-based, and power-based regime theories), the increasing role of non-state actors and the importance of broader (non-regime) economic factors and forces in particular have changed the way we conceive of the whereabouts of the global politics of climate change, how they are conducted, and for whom.[44] We return to discuss these issues in more depth in Chapters 3, 4, and 5.

Notes

1 Joanna Depledge, *The Organization of Global Negotiations: Constructing the Climate Regime* (London: Earthscan, 2005).
2 Matthew Paterson and Michael Grubb, "The International Politics of Climate Change," *International Affairs* 68, no. 2 (1992): 293–310.
3 Peter Newell, *Climate for Change: Non-State Actors and the Global Politics of the Greenhouse* (Cambridge: Cambridge University Press, 2000).
4 Bas Arts, *The Political Influence of Global NGOs: Case Studies on the Climate and Biodiversity Conventions* (Utrecht, the Netherlands: International Books, 1998); Peter Newell, *Climate for Change*.
5 Michele Betsill and Elisabeth Corell, eds, *NGO Diplomacy: The Influence of Nongovernmental Organizations in International Environmental Negotiations* (Cambridge, Mass.: MIT Press, 2008), 3.
6 Kathrin Dombrowski, "Filling the gap? An Analysis of NGO Responses to Participation and Representation Deficits in Global Climate Governance," *Paper prepared for the Amsterdam Conference on the Human Dimension of Global Environmental Change*, December 2–4, 2009.
7 United Nations, *United Nations Framework Convention on Climate Change*, Bonn, Germany: UNFCCC Secretariat, 1992, available online at http://unfccc. int/resource/docs/convkp/conveng.pdf [accessed January 19, 2015].
8 Michael Grubb with Christiaan Vrolijk and Duncan Brack, *The Kyoto Protocol: A Guide and Assessment* (London: Earthscan and the Royal Institute of International Affairs, 1999).

9   Michael Grubb and Farhana Yamin, "Climatic Collapse at The Hague: What Happened, Why, and Where Do We Go From Here?" *International Affairs* 77, no. 2 (2001): 261–76.

10 Chukwumerije Okereke, Phillip Mann, and Andy Newsham, "Assessment of Key Negotiating Issues at Nairobi Climate COP/MOP and What it Means For the Future of the Climate Regime," *Tyndall Centre Working Paper* 106 (2007).

11 Benito Muller, "Bali 2007: On the Road Again! Impressions from the Thirteenth UN Climate Change Conference," available online at http://www.oxfordclimatepolicy.org/publications/documents/comment_0208-2.pdf [accessed January 19, 2015]; Jennifer Morgan, "Towards a New Global Climate Deal: An analysis of the Agreements and Politics of the Bali Negotiations. E3G," available online at http://www.e3g.org/images/uploads/Bali_Analysis_Morgan_080120.pdf [accessed January 19, 2015].

12 United Nations Environmental Programme, *The Emissions Gap Report 2013* (Nairobi: UNEP, 2013).

13 United Nations Environmental Programme, *Bridging the Emissions Gap* (Nairobi: UNEP, 2011).

14 Hans Joachim Schellnhuber, Bill Hare, Olivia Serdeczny, Michiel Schaeffer, Sophie Adams, Florent Baarsch, Susanne Schwan, Dim Coumou, Alexander Robinson, Marion Vieweg, Franziska Piontek, Reik Donner, Jakob Runge, Kira Rehfeld, Joeri Rogelj, Mahe Perrette, Arathy Menon, Carl-Friedrich Schleussner, Alberte Bondeau, Anastasia Svirejeva-Hopkins, Jacob Schewe, Katja Frieler, Lila Warszawski, and Marcia Rocha, *Turn Down the Heat: Climate Extremes, Regional Impacts, and the Case for Resilience* (Washington, DC: World Bank, 2013).

15 Bert Bolin, "Scientific Assessment of Climate Change," in *International Politics of Climate Change: Key Issues and Actors,* ed. Gunnar Fermann (Oslo, Norway: Scandinavian University Press, 1997), 99.

16 Michel Foucault, *Power/Knowledge: Selected Interviews and Other Writings 1972–77* (New York: Pantheon books, 1980), 27.

17 Bolin, "Scientific Assessment of Climate Change," 102.

18 Peter Haas, *Saving the Mediterranean: The Politics of International Environmental Cooperation* (New York: Columbia University Press, 1990).

19 Karen Litfin, *Ozone Discourses* (New York: Columbia University Press, 1994).

20 Sonia Boehmer-Christiansen, "Global Climate Protection Policy: The Limits of Scientific Advice – Part 1," *Global Environmental Change* 4, no. 2 (1992): 140–59.

21 Among the most prominent "climate skeptics" are Fred Singer (George Mason University) and Richard Linzen (MIT).

22 Fred Pearce, *The Climate Files: The Battle for the Truth about Global Warming* (London: Guardian books, 2010).

23 "US Reportedly Seeking To Sink Watson as IPCC Head," available online at http://business-humanrights.org/en/climate-change-us-reportedly-seeking-to-sink-watson-as-ipcc-head-0#c16018 [accessed January 19, 2015].

24 Article 2 of the UNFCCC (1992): available online at http://unfccc.int/resource/docs/convkp/conveng.pdf [accessed January 19, 2015].

25 *ECO* NGO Newsletter, issue 7, Geneva, 1990.

26 Adil Najam, Saleemul Huq, and Youba Sokona, "Climate Negotiations Beyond Kyoto: Developing Countries, Concerns and Interests," *Climate Policy* 3, no. 3 (2003): 221–31; Michele Williams, "The Third World and Global Environmental Negotiations: Interests, Institutions and Ideas," *Global Environmental Politics* 5, no. 3 (2005): 48–9.

27 Anil Argwal and Sunita Narain, *"Global Warming in an Unequal World: A Case of Environmental Colonialism,"* (New Delhi, India: Centre for Science and the Environment/WRI, 1991).

28 Article 3 of the UNFCCC (1992): available online at http://unfccc.int/resource/docs/convkp/conveng.pdf [accessed January 19, 2015].

29 Zoe Young, *A New Green Order? The World Bank and the Politics of the Global Environment Facility* (London: Pluto Press, 2002).

30 Sjur Kasa, Anne Therese Gullberg, and Gørild Heggelund, "The Group of 77 in the International Climate Negotiations: Recent Developments and Future Directions," *International Environmental Agreements: Politics, Law and Economics* 8, no. 2 (2008): 113–27.

31 Scott Barrett, "Montreal Versus Kyoto: International Cooperation on the Global Environment," in *Global Public Goods,* eds Inge Kaul, Isabelle Grunberg, and Marc Stern (New York: Oxford University Press, 1999), 192–220.

32 J. Timmons Roberts and Bradley Parks, *A Climate of Injustice: Global Inequality, North–South Politics and Climate Policy* (Cambridge, Mass.: MIT Press, 2007).

33 Peter Newell and Matthew Paterson, *Climate Capitalism: Global Warming and the Transformation of the Global Economy* (Cambridge: Cambridge University Press, 2010); Peter Newell, Max Boykoff, and Emily Boyd, eds, *The New Carbon Economy: Constitution, Governance and Contestation* (Oxford: Wiley and Sons, 2012).

34 UNFCCC (2012) *UNFCCC releases report on the benefits of the Kyoto Protocol's clean development mechanism.* Bonn: UNFCCC press office, November 20, available online at http://cdm.unfccc.int/CDMNews/issues/issues/I_KYD6PO19YS9DE7YGH894BJ9WRBCQ4Z/viewnewsitem.html [accessed January 19, 2015].

35 World Bank, *Development and Climate Change,* World Development Report 2010 (Washington, DC: World Bank, 2010).

36 Matthew Hoffman, *Climate Governance at the Crossroads: Experimenting with a Global Response after Kyoto* (Oxford: Oxford University Press, 2011); Naomi Klein, *This Changes Everything: Capitalism vs The Climate* (London: Simon and Schuster, 2014).

37 Jan-Peter Voss, "Innovation Processes in Governance: the Development of 'Emissions Trading' as a New Policy instrument," *Science and Public Policy* 34, no. 5 (2007): 329–43; Jon Birger Skjærseth and Jørgen Wettestad, *EU Emissions Trading: Initiation, Decision Making and Implementation* (Aldershot, UK: Ashgate, 2008).

38 Pilita Clark, "UN-led carbon market 'close to collapse,'" *Financial Times,* October 2, 2012, www.ft.com/cms/s/0/ee81799c-0c84-11e2-a776-00144-feabdc0.html.

39 Tanya Gilbertson and Oscar Reyes, *Carbon Trading: How it Works and Why it Fails* (Uppsala: Dag Hammarskjold Foundation, 2009).

40 Miranda Schreurs and Elizabeth Economy, eds, *The Internationalization of Environmental Protection* (Cambridge: Cambridge University Press, 1997); Peter Newell, "The Political Economy of Global Environmental Governance," *Review of International Studies* 34 (July 2008): 507–29.
41 Philipp Pattberg and Johannes Stripple, "Beyond the Public and Private Divide: Remapping Transnational Climate Governance in the 21st century," *International Environmental Agreements* 8, no. 4 (2008): 367–88.
42 Newell, *Climate for Change*.
43 Robert Keohane and David Victor, "The Regime Complex for Climate Change," *Discussion paper* 2010-33 (Cambridge, Mass: Harvard Project on International Climate Agreements, 2010).
44 David Levy and Peter Newell, eds, *The Business of Global Environmental Governance* (Cambridge, Mass.: MIT Press, 2005); Chukwumerije Okereke, Harriet Bulkeley, and Heike Schroeder, "Conceptualizing Climate Governance Beyond the International Regime," *Global Environmental Politics* 9, no. 1 (2009): 58–78.

2

GOVERNANCE FOR WHOM?

Equity, justice, and the politics of sustainable development

In this chapter, we examine issues of equity and justice in the governance of climate change. As we saw in Chapter 1, from concerns about responsibility for causing the problem and the allocation of the burden of responding to it through to questions of climate adaptation, issues of equity and justice run through every aspect of the governance of climate change. Unsurprisingly, therefore, many activists explicitly invoke the language of "climate justice" when campaigning on these issues.[1]

Picking up from Chapter 1, we place the issue of climate change within the broader context of shifting North–South relations as well as exploring its links to key development concerns around aid, debt, energy, and trade, and the ways in which efforts to tackle climate change can be made compatible with the alleviation of poverty. This comes amid growing emphasis on "climate-compatible development": lower carbon models of development that are resilient to the effects of climate change and help lift poorer people out of poverty.[2] As with other chapters in this book, we suggest that addressing climate change is in reality a subset of wider governance processes which shape, and at the same time are affected by, the nature of climate governance. We look in turn at three key areas where these issues come to the fore: the question of responsibility; the question of who pays for action on mitigation and adaptation; and the question of who bears the costs of actions and inactions. We conclude by summarizing some of the key governance challenges that confront efforts to address issues of justice and equity in relation to climate change.

Whose responsibility? Global warming in an unequal world

Historical and contemporary relations of inequity and injustice form a powerful frame by which poorer countries and peoples make sense of climate change as a political issue.[3] Histories of suspicion, distrust, and inequity are played out in the contemporary politics of climate change, accounting for conflicting notions of whom climate governance should serve and how. Whether it is claims about ecological debt or climate justice, there is a powerful sense in which climate change has the potential to further aggravate inequalities within and between societies.[4] This sense of injustice derives from the fact that those who have contributed least to the problem of climate change in the past, including most of the world's poor, are those most susceptible to its worst effects now and in the future. Meanwhile, richer countries are better placed to adapt to the climate impacts that they will suffer. Statements by leaders from developing countries illustrate the strength of feeling on the issue. In 2008 President Museveni of Uganda described climate change as "an act of aggression by the rich against the poor."[5] Meanwhile, in March 2003, Ambassador Lionel Hurst, speaking on behalf of the small island states, said:

> the most populous and wealthiest of the world face a moral challenge greater than colonialism or slavery. They are failing in that challenge. Men [sic] have lost reason in the fossil fuel economy . . . Inhabitants of small islands have not agreed [to be] sacrificial lambs on the altar of the wealth of the rich.[6]

Other critics have picked up on the issue of developing countries being reconstituted as a sink for GHG emissions from developed countries through the "flexibility mechanisms," most critically referred to as "carbon colonialism."[7] Even senior government officials within the climate change negotiations such as Raúl Estrada-Oyuela, then chairman of the Ad Hoc Group on the Berlin Mandate (AGBM), noted at the time of the Kyoto agreement:

> My reservation was that the CDM is considered a form of joint implementation but I don't understand how a commitment can be jointly implemented if only one of the parties involved is committed to limit emissions and the other party is free from a qualitative point of view. Such disparity has been at the root of every colonization since the time of the Greeks.[8]

The geographies of responsibility have shifted significantly, however, since the early days of the climate regime, as we saw in Chapter 1. While the G77 is able to speak with one voice in demanding further action from the developed countries, it contains among its members the world's largest current contributor to climate change (China) and many other countries whose emission trajectories are starting to match those of the United States, the European Union, and Japan (such as India, Brazil, and Mexico). The top five emitters of CO_2 are now China (29 percent), the United States (16 percent), the European Union (11 percent), India (6 percent), and the Russian Federation (5 percent), followed by Japan (4 percent). Indeed, CO_2 emissions from the Organization for Economic Cooperation and Development (OECD) countries now account for only one third of global emissions.[9] At issue here is the extent to which "differentiated responsibilities" should reflect past, current, or future trends of GHG emissions. Any new international agreement that emerges in Paris in 2015 that involves these industrializing countries will have to acknowledge their historically low contributions to the problem even if current levels now match those of developed countries. This is because much of today's climate change has been caused by emissions generated principally by the development of the global North. In this sense, the North continues to owe a huge "ecological debt" to the South, having consumed a disproportionate share of its global and historical entitlement. Furthermore, developing countries continue to be home to a significant percentage of the world's poor and their per capita contributions to the problem are dwarfed by those of the United States, for example, which is home to just 4 percent of the world's population but is responsible for 20 percent of global emissions of all GHGs (not just CO_2), while 136 developing countries are together responsible for 24 percent of those emissions. It becomes clear that the issue of inequity in per capita emissions goes beyond national borders when we consider that the richest 20 percent of the world's population is responsible for over 60 percent of current emissions of GHG.[10] Taking into account the inequity between and within countries concerning per capita contributions to climate change will be a significant challenge for future international agreements.

Beyond the generic framing of common but differentiated responsibility in the UNFCCC, a variety of proposals have been advanced that seek to tackle the thorny issue of per capita emissions and to recognize and reconcile the right to development with the need to dramatically reduce emissions. "Contraction and Convergence" is one such proposal, developed by a small London-based NGO called the Global Commons Institute. The basic idea, which underpins the proposal, is that developed countries have to contract their emissions down towards an agreed level which would address the UNFCCC's aim of avoiding dangerous interference in the climate system, while poorer developing countries would be allowed to increase their emissions up to the agreed level. Per capita entitlements would then be bought and sold to harness the market towards this climate stabilization goal. The idea has many opponents, not least the United States and other larger polluters who insist that permits would have to be allocated based on existing need (a grandfathering system) rather than a per capita basis which would favor developing countries. The idea that everyone has equal access to the global commons has powerful political and moral purchase, however.

Another proposal is the Greenhouse Development Rights framework developed by the Stockholm Environment Institute, Christian Aid, and the Heinrich Böll foundation. It aims to promote the right to development in a carbon-constrained world while holding warming below 2 °C, a task which may already seem impossible.[11] Countries' abatement targets would be calculated by the number of people above a development threshold (US$20 a day): the "global consuming class" as they refer to it. Responsibility and capacity indicators (gross domestic product (GDP), population, cumulative emissions), including income available after meeting basic needs, are used in the calculations. Such an approach helps to go beyond aggregated national figures of wealth and development, challenging divisions made between countries such as that of "Annex 1" and "non-Annex 1," or "developed" and "developing" countries, while also providing a quantitative handle on how to assess obligations to tackle climate change. Implementation of such an approach could be through taxation into a global fund for redistribution for mitigation and adaptation, or via national mitigation targets as set out in the Kyoto Protocol. Questions remain about whether this proposal is politically realistic, and as such it does not provide a way of bypassing conflicts over how money would be redistributed or by whom, or how capacity and responsibility indicators would be agreed. Nonetheless, such proposals show that it is possible to conceive of responsibility for climate change in different ways, with significant implications for the development of climate policy and its ability to address issues of equity.

Such debates are slowly taking shape within the international arena. Although the 2007 Bali Action Plan places emphasis on "nationally appropriate mitigation actions" in less developed (non-Annex 1) countries, the question of how to attribute responsibility for emissions remains hotly contested. In addition to the challenges of historical and future emissions, nation-based or per capita emissions allocations, a further concern is where along global supply networks responsibility for emissions should be allocated—whether the point of production or consumption is the appropriate focus.[12] Many rapidly industrializing countries such as China claim their emissions profile is a by-product of demand for low-cost manufactured goods in developed countries. In other words, they should not be penalized for the fact that many countries are able to outsource the most carbon and energy-intensive stages of the production process to parts of the world where it is cheapest to do so.

If climate politics could ever have been characterized as at core a conflict between North and South over responsibility, the rise of these issues on the agenda means that the picture is certainly more complex now. The issues around which developing countries once mobilized have changed, as the political and economic might of those who once relied upon the solidarity of other states as part of the G77 coalition has increased. It is increasingly difficult for the BRICS countries (Brazil, Russia, India, China, and South Africa) to argue that they should not have obligations to control their emissions of GHG as their net contributions to the problem match those of countries which are obliged to do so, as we saw above. Likewise, growing reliance upon flexible mechanisms and market-based instruments has served to fragment the opposition of developing countries to involving themselves in emission reductions projects. The GRILA (Group of Latin American countries) has seen opportunities to access funds for forestry projects that might not otherwise be supported within the G77. Given this diversity, it is unsurprising that speaking as a united bloc makes increasingly less sense for developing countries in the climate negotiations. Some of the more powerful governments have been drawn into alternative governance forums for reaching agreements on climate change. The preference among India, China, and Brazil is to conclude bilateral deals and engage in partnerships that offer more immediate returns alongside, and some suggest in competition with, Kyoto. Over time, these have included the Asia–Pacific Partnership on Clean Development and Climate, the Renewable Energy and Energy Efficiency Partnership (REEEP), the Australia–China Partnership, the EU–China Partnership on Climate Change, the US–India bilateral agreement on nuclear energy, and agreements on EU–India energy cooperation. As India, China, and Brazil find alternative paths for addressing climate change we are perhaps left in the international negotiating arena with an "insecure alliance between the unwilling (OPEC) and the powerless (least developed countries) providing few impulses towards increasing G77 flexibility in the post-Kyoto negotiations."[13] The new geographies of responsibility for climate change are therefore not only shaping the trajectory of current and future international climate agreements, but can be seen as one of the factors shaping the emergence of a whole range of new governance arenas for addressing climate change, a topic to which we return in Chapter 3.

Who pays?

A second key issue that has shaped the North–South politics of climate change is the concern about who should meet the costs of addressing the issue. Agreeing a fair and equitable allocation of responsibility for acting on climate change requires subsequent agreement about who pays for such actions and how. In governance terms, some of the key conflicts are about which institutions should oversee such flows of funds from North to South, and on what terms. As we saw in Chapter 1, the battle over whether the GEF should be the body to oversee aid and technology transfer reflects concerns about the role of the World Bank, with whom many developing countries have had, and continue to have, difficult relations. We also noted how this contest was replayed over the role of the World Bank in managing the Green Climate Fund. A further concern, illustrating how broader North–South politics have shaped climate governance, is where the finance for climate change will come from. Reflecting a deep-seated fear that existing aid budgets might be diverted to fund climate change measures, the obligations for Annex 1 parties explicitly call on them to provide "new and additional" financial resources, though the extent to which this has been the case is hotly contested.

Turning first to questions of institutional oversight, it is clear that multilateral and regional development banks such as the Asian Development Bank have sought to define for themselves a key role in financing mitigation and adaptation based on a recognition that climate change can reverse development gains in so many other areas where they work. A key actor here is the World Bank. In addition to being an implementing agency of the GEF, the financing agency for the climate agreements, the World Bank has been involved in a range of climate change initiatives. Though there are now more than 20 different bilateral and multilateral funds for climate change, the Climate Investment Funds (CIFs) of the World Bank represent more public finance than has ever before been dedicated to climate change. A key role the World Bank seeks to perform is the provision of incentives for the private sector to carry some of the burden of funding climate protection. Piloting and demonstrating sustainable energy projects helps to minimize some of the risks that deter private actors from investing in the poorest areas of the world. For example, the Scaling up Renewable Energy Program was launched at the Copenhagen climate summit in 2009 with the aim of catalyzing new economic opportunities for private sector investment in renewable energy production in low income countries, while the World Bank's Clean Technology Fund identifies its niche in terms of providing finance to developing countries at more concessional rates than the standard multilateral development banks' terms, and at the scale necessary to help provide them with incentives to integrate low-carbon strategies into their development plans and investment decisions.[14]

Perhaps more significantly still, the World Bank, as trustee, has been charged with interim management of the Green Climate Fund called for by the Copenhagen Accord to oversee the distribution of US$100 billion per year for climate change mitigation and adaptation. The design of the Fund was approved at COP 17 in Durban, South Africa, in 2011 and was meant to be operational in 2013. According to developed country self-reporting, as of 2014, over US$30 billion has been delivered as fast-start finance, the bulk of which is made up of more than US$10 billion from aid and development agencies, US$6 billion from investment promotion and export credit agencies, and US$6 billion from multilateral climate change funds.[15]

However, while some parts of the World Bank are promoting action on climate change, many other policies pursued by the same institution—notably energy market deregulation—do not take their impact on climate change into account. For example, the World Bank concedes that "unregulated electricity markets are likely to put renewable energy technologies at a disadvantage in the short-run because they favor the cheapest energy as determined purely by price, but do not capture environmental and social externalities."[16] This raises the critical question of whether climate concerns are being mainstreamed into core World Bank activities. One report found that less than 30 percent of the World Bank's lending to the energy sector has integrated climate considerations into project decision making. As late as 2007, more than 50 percent of the World Bank's US$1.8 billion energy-sector portfolio did not include climate change considerations at all.[17] Indeed, from 2006 to 2010, the World Bank increased its lending towards fossil fuel-based projects by 400 percent.[18] On this basis, it is clear that climate change has yet to be mainstreamed throughout the activities of the World Bank.

Whatever their limitations may be, development banks do have a key role to play in supporting clean energy transitions in the developing world. Energy is clearly pivotal to development, and meeting the development needs of the majority of the world's people in a carbon-constrained world presents a global challenge of staggering proportions. Today, 1.6 billion people are without electricity. Electricity demand in developing countries is projected to increase three to five times over the next 30 years,[19] and 57 percent of future power sector investment will occur in developing countries.[20] Without a significant change of course, most of this will be fossil fuel-based electricity production that will exacerbate climate change. A recent UN report notes that of the "substantial shifts in investment patterns" required to mitigate climate change, "half of these should occur in developing countries which will require incentives and support for policy formulation and implementation."[21] Effective governance of these broader processes will clearly be key to the success of any efforts at climate change governance.

In this context, the second issue concerning who pays is how to generate new sources of funding. To address the question of where the money will come from, a High Level Advisory Group on Climate Change Finance was convened in 2010 and recommended a series of potential funding sources including a carbon price of around US\$20–25 per ton of CO_2 equivalent by 2020, carbon taxes, taxes on shipping and aviation, a financial transaction tax, redeployment of fossil fuel subsidies, the use of carbon markets, and a key role for multilateral development banks in levering public and private finance along the lines discussed above.[22]

There is increasing emphasis upon the need to expand the amount of private investment in addressing climate change in particular. A UNFCCC report on investment and financial flows to address climate change argues that the "carbon market . . . would have to be significantly expanded to address needs for additional investment and financial flows."[23] Indeed, the Adaptation Fund is in large part financed by sales of certified emission reductions under the UN's Clean Development Mechanism. The share of proceeds amounts to 2 percent of the value of Certified Emission Reductions issued each year for CDM projects, contributing to the more than US\$226 million which the fund has allocated to 39 countries around the world.[24]

In approaches to financing climate change mitigation, growing attention is being paid to the need to capture co-benefits in developing countries: projects that deliver climate and development dividends simultaneously. In line with this argument, the CDM is often highlighted as a great development opportunity for developing countries to use climate related funds to invest in projects and technologies that benefit the poor. The projects it approves are meant to capture social and environmental benefits as well as deliver emission reductions additional to those that would have been funded anyway. However, in reality, investment has tended to flow to larger developing countries such as China and India that between them are currently home to over 70 percent of all registered CDM projects and not, for example, to Africa, where just over 2 percent of projects are currently registered. There has also been a neglect of broader sustainable development benefits flowing from the projects even if they are successful at reducing the growth of GHG emissions, partly because these benefits are not monetarized in the same way emission reductions are monetarized through the allocation of Certified Emissions Reductions.[25] In governance terms, there are also issues of limited capacity to manage project demand in some countries, as well as to oversee and implement the projects in a way which protects not just the interests of the investor but also the communities which host these projects.[26] We discuss these issues in further depth in Chapters 5 and 6. For the moment, it is sufficient to note that the debate concerning where additional funds for addressing climate change should come from is far from being resolved in terms of either policy or practice, with significant concern expressed that addressing climate change may serve to divert much needed resources away from other environment and development agendas, will be tokenistic at best, and may serve to promote particular solutions to the climate change problem favored by the developed world rather than those developing countries in receipt of climate finance.

There is also the danger of trying to create islands of formal climate governance in a sea of unregulated, ungoverned flows of trade and finance, unguided by the imperative of addressing climate change. For example, the implemented and scheduled emission trading schemes and carbon taxes thus far only put a carbon price on approximately 7 percent of global emissions.[27] Moreover, only a small percentage of trade, aid, production, and finance is governed by public bodies charged with tackling climate change.[28] Official Development Assistance (ODA) funds are currently less than 1 percent of investment globally.[29] What this highlights is the pressing need to identify policies, strategies, and interventions which are able to steer financial flows, public and private, to where they are most needed but in ways that are consistent with the goal of reducing GHG emissions. For those countries most integrated within the global trading system (OECD and BRICS), one avenue that has been advocated is an agreement on trade in energy services and the use of energy-intensity indicators. For example, proposals for an energy round in the World Trade Organization (WTO) aimed at meeting the energy needs of the poor through access to services and technologies are justified in the following way:

> Facilitating access to products and services in this area can help improve energy efficiency, reduce greenhouse gas emissions and have a positive impact on air quality, water, soil and natural resources conservation. A successful outcome of the negotiations on environmental goods and services could deliver a triple-win for WTO members: a win for the environment, a win for trade and a win for development.[30]

According to the World Bank, the removal of tariffs for four basic clean energy technologies (solar, wind, clean coal, and efficient lighting) in 18 developing countries with high levels of GHG emissions would result in trade gains of up to 7 percent. The removal of both tariffs and non-tariff barriers could boost trade by as much as 13 percent.[31] For others, such as countries in sub-Saharan Africa which are less well integrated into the global economy and more aid-dependent, important support can be provided by donors to enable clean energy transitions. The World Bank and regional development banks, meanwhile, can play a key role in screening public and private flows going into countries that are already attractive investment locations, as well as provide inducements that reduce the risk of investors entering new markets in parts of Asia, Africa, and Latin America that have not received such flows to date.

What this more positive analysis overlooks is the climate impacts of increased trade and the simultaneous and ongoing levels of donor support for fossil fuels, as noted previously. For example, a narrow focus on specific sectoral gains ignores the way in which unfettered trade liberalization in general serves to place the global economy on a collision course with the goal of reducing GHG emissions because of the huge increases in emissions associated with transporting large volumes of goods over greater distances.[32]

Who bears the costs?

In justice and equity terms it is necessary to relate the question of who pays for action in financial terms to the question of who bears the costs of climate change, not just in terms of biophysical impacts, but also the human and social costs of how the issue is currently governed, or conversely, "ungoverned."

The findings contained in the 2014 IPCC report on the impacts of climate change demonstrate quite clearly that poorer and marginalized communities in drought-prone areas, those experiencing water scarcity, or those whose livelihoods depend on agriculture will be the worst affected and have the least capacity to adapt to climate change. As IPCC lead author Neil Adger notes, "the impacts of climate change are likely to be greater on those countries more dependent on primary sector economic activities [mostly farming], primarily because of the increase in uncertainty on productivity in the primary sectors."[33] As shown in Box 2.1, changes in the supply of water, natural resources, and food bring in their wake enormous social changes and disruptions. Across the developing countries, it is areas of sub-Saharan Africa, where poverty is most acute, that will be worst affected. Indeed, a multidonor report *Poverty and Climate Change* rightly acknowledges that "Climate change is a serious risk to poverty reduction and threatens to undo decades of development efforts."[34]

BOX 2.1 CLIMATE CHANGE AND POVERTY

- Food production needs to double to meet the needs of an additional 3 billion people over the next 30 years. Climate change is projected to decrease agricultural productivity in the tropics and sub-tropics.
- One-third of the world's population is susceptible to water scarcity. Populations facing water scarcity will more than double over the next 30 years. Climate change is projected to decrease water availability in many (semi-) arid regions.
- Wood fuel is the main source of fuel for one-third of the world's population. Wood fuel demand is expected to double in the next 50 years. Climate change will make forest management more difficult due to increases in pests and fires.
- Today 1.6 billion people are without electricity. Electricity demand in developing countries will increase three to five times over the next 30 years. Fossil fuel-based electricity production will exacerbate climate change.

Source: Ogunlade Davidson, Kirsten Halsnæs, Saleemul Huq, Marcel Kok, Bert Metz, Youba Sokona, and Jan Verhagen, "The Development and Climate Nexus: The Case of Sub-Saharan Africa," *Climate Policy* 3, no.1 (2003): 97–113.

Given the slow pace of progress of international cooperation on climate change, noted in Chapter 1, and the difficulties of advancing some of the mitigation options discussed above amid conflicts about how and by whom they should be governed, attention has increasingly turned to the issue of adaptation to climate change. Vulnerability to climate change cuts across geographical boundaries and it is often the poor in all parts of the world that are affected most, raising issues of distributive justice. We saw in the case of Hurricane Katrina in 2005 how poorer communities of color bear some of the worst devastation inflicted by "natural" disasters. Poorer people often have the least means of adapting their livelihoods and means of survival to sudden change of the sort associated with extreme weather events. Bradley Parks and Timmons Roberts argue, for example, that Hurricane

Mitch in Honduras "serves as a parable about uneven vulnerability to global climate change."[35] The Economic Commission for Latin America and the Caribbean (ECLAC) estimated that US$5 billion would be necessary to fund reconstruction efforts, to say nothing of damage to the banana plantations that were so central to generating export revenues. These revenues fell to one fifth of their pre-hurricane levels, forcing Dole and Chiquita to lay off 25,000 workers and setting in train a series of other devastating social consequences. Likewise, the torrential rains and tropical cyclones which struck Mozambique and surrounding countries in 1999 left 700 people dead, one million people displaced, and extensive losses of land, animals, and other means of survival leaving a reconstruction bill of US$700 million.[36] Heat waves in Europe, wildfires in the United States, droughts in Australia, and deadly flooding in Thailand and Pakistan, as well as Typhoon Haiyan in 2013 and Superstorm Sandy in 2012, have further drawn attention to the devastating effects of climate change. Constructing effective mechanisms of adaptation raises issues not just of distributive but also of procedural justice.[37]

The concern with issues of procedural justice reflects the fact that the impacts are felt and costs borne by poorer groups in particular, not just as a result of climate change and differential ability to adapt to it, but because of the ways in which mitigation and adaptation policies are designed and implemented. Though the UN climate change negotiations may seem far removed from local land conflicts, the governance of climate change intersects with the governance of other key resources such as water and land.[38] For example, there have been cases of negative impacts on the poor when land is given up for carbon sink purposes, giving rise to accusations of carbon colonialism. One Norwegian company operating in Uganda that leased its lands for a sequestration project is said to have resulted in the eviction of 8,000 people in 13 villages.[39] The project in Bukaleba Forestry Reserve was meant to offset GHG emissions of a coal-fired power plant to be built in Norway.[40] Likewise, carbon finance can provide a financial lifeline to the operation of landfill sites, which poorer communities had been campaigning to close down but whose life is extended because of the profit to be made from capturing and burning methane.[41]

People do not meekly accept their fate as victims of forms of climate governance they consider unjust, however. There is significant resistance to attempts at "accumulation by de-carbonization" by communities and movements resisting the commodification and inequities produced by "green grabs" of their land.[42] Acting as watchdogs, NGOs have also played an important role in monitoring public and private activity in the new carbon economy, and drawing attention to the inequities it produces or fails to address. SinksWatch, for example, an initiative of the World Rainforest Movement (WRM) set up in 2001, monitors the impact of the financing and creation of sinks projects to highlight the threat they pose to forests and other ecosystems, to forest peoples as well as to the climate. A particular concern is the exclusion of marginalized groups from their own forest resources once they become the property of a distant carbon trader for whom they represent a valuable investment opportunity. One case in point is the Plantar project which involves planting 23,100 hectares of eucalyptus tree plantations to produce wood for charcoal, which will then be used in pig iron production instead of coal. The project also claims carbon credits for sequestration of carbon through the trees planted. Because of the social and environmental impacts of the project, over 50 Brazilian NGOs, movements, churches, and trade unions have been urging investors to refrain from buying carbon credits originating from the project.[43]

In the search for means of protecting poorer groups from the effects of climate change or the effects of poorly conceived forms of climate governance, many affected communities and activities have increasingly turned to the language and tools of human rights. As Kevin Watkins of the United Nations Development Programme (UNDP) said of climate change: "it is about social justice and the human rights of the world's poor and marginalized. Failure to act on climate change would be tantamount to a systematic violation of the human rights of the poor."[44] As a mechanism for seeking redress for rights violations, access to the law is limited for many poorer groups, but there have been a series of legal cases which seek to explore the boundaries of culpability and establish new and challenging legal precedents.[45] One such case involves the Inuit community in North America. On December 7, 2005, the Inuit Circumpolar Conference (ICC) submitted a "Petition to the Inter-American Commission on Human Rights Seeking Relief from Violations Resulting from Global Warming caused by Acts and Omissions of the United States." The United States was targeted as the world's largest contributor to GHG emissions. Sheila Watt-Cloutier, Inuk woman and chair of the ICC, submitted the petition on behalf of herself, 62 other named individuals, "and all Inuit of the Arctic regions of the United States and Canada who have been affected by the impacts of climate change."[46] The petition calls on the Inter-American Commission on Human Rights to investigate the harm caused to the Inuit by global warming, and to declare the United States in violation of rights affirmed in the 1948 American Declaration of the Rights and Duties of Man and other instruments of international law such as the International Convention on Civil and Political Rights and the International Convention on Economic, Social, and Cultural Rights. Specifically, the petition alleges:

> The impacts of climate change, caused by acts and omissions by the United States, violate the Inuit's fundamental human rights protected by the American Declaration of the Rights and Duties of Man and other international instruments. These include their rights to the benefits of culture, to property, to the preservation of health, life, physical integrity, security and a means of subsistence and to residence, movement, and the inviolability of the home.[47]

The Commission rejected the petition as inadmissible, though reasons for the refusal were not given. Importantly, however, the human rights issues raised by the case were not disputed by the Commission. One positive outcome of the case has been that the Commission invited petitioners to request a public hearing on the matter which took place on March 1, 2007.

Civil society actors in both North and South also have a key role to play in debates about equity and justice in climate governance through enhancing the voice and reach of excluded groups. This can take the form of legal groups—such as the UK-based FIELD—helping to redress some of the procedural inequities, which mean levels of participation and effective engagement from smaller developing countries in the climate negotiations are low. Outside the formal negotiating arenas of climate governance, it includes the climate justice movement which draws attention to the disproportionate impact of climate change on the poor. This movement focuses on the way in which climate change has the potential to exacerbate existing social inequalities and draws much of its critique from broader contestations of neo-liberal globalization. For the activists spearheading the movement, climate justice means:

> holding fossil fuel corporations accountable for the central role they play in contributing to global warming . . . challenging these companies at every level – from the production and marketing of fossil fuels themselves, to their underhanded political influence, to their PR prowess, to the unjust "solutions" they propose, to the fossil fuel-based globalization they are driving.[48]

The movement works through popular education and protest and seeks to provide a space for the articulation of claims by those most affected by climate change, but who contribute least to the problem. It has also spawned new alliances such as the "Stop Climate Chaos" coalition involving environment and development NGOs working on climate justice issues and wanting to draw attention to impacts on the poor in particular.[49]

Governance issues and challenges

From this discussion of the politics of responsibility, costs, and burdens of climate change we find that there are a number of cross-cutting governance issues and challenges that arise. First, battles over the definition of the nature of the problem of climate change affect how and where it is addressed. In this chapter we have seen how action on climate change has been presented as a trade opportunity by some (and as barrier to trade by others), and how it has got caught up in, and at the same time redefines, older debates about issues of aid and development. As connections to other issues and policy arenas are made, new actors are enrolled in climate governance from trade and financial institutions to bodies dealing with human rights and development. The new resources being made available to tackle climate change attract international organizations, civil society groups, and business alike. Carbon entrepreneurs seek a share of the market while development NGOs define for themselves a role in addressing climate change, and international agencies from UNDP to the United Nations Industrial Development Organization (UNIDO) line up alongside the World Bank to make sure their presence is felt and their expertise brought to bear.

Just as each of these actors seeks to define the nature of the problem in a way which advances their interests, so too they compete to define appropriate solutions. In particular, the privileging of market-based solutions reflects the interests of particular organizations and nation-states with their neo-liberal emphasis on using the market and allocating property rights to create incentives to reduce emissions wherever it is cheapest to do so. The proliferation of actors and sites of climate governance also raises significant challenges in terms of policy coordination and coherence. Instead of coordinated strategies between global bodies working in relevant areas and across levels of governance from local government up to the global, we find high levels of incoherence. The activities of one body or set of organizations can systematically undermine those of others. New trade agreements increase the transport of goods over longer distances, adding to the emissions that climate negotiators are struggling to reduce,[50] while multilateral development bank-lending supports projects that commit vast amounts of GHG to the atmosphere. For instance, the World Bank, in a move that attracted widespread criticism from civil society, made a loan of US$3.75

billion to the South African national utility Eskom, the largest stand-alone energy investment in the Bank's history, to finance the construction of the 4,800 MW Medupi supercritical coal-fired power plant.

We have seen in this chapter that whereas once climate change was an issue mainly addressed by the UN, its nature as a political issue at the intersection of the relationship between economy, energy, and environment means that it touches many other policy areas which in turn shape the effectiveness of action on climate change. This close interweaving of climate change with other key sectors of the economy raises another important issue, that of the "un-governance" of climate change: issues and areas of active and deliberate neglect. These are areas of politics and practice which are often not considered as climate policy, but which contribute significantly to the problem around energy, transport, agriculture and trade, for example. This requires us to look not only at the activities of governments, but also at the international institutions and market actors that shape so strongly the direction of national development strategies.

Second, this chapter has shown how new sites for climate governance become venues for the articulation of demands that it has not been possible to achieve by other means or in other forums. The forging of links to aid, debt, and trade issues illustrates this clearly. While some have sought to maintain clear boundaries around climate governance for fear of overloading the agenda with the politics of these other issues and hence slowing progress, these new sites for climate governance also open up new potential avenues for advancing action. While the interlinkages between different policy issues create a challenge in terms of the governability of the "regime complex" around climate change, positive benefits might be able to be achieved from such synergies.[51] The emergence of new sites of climate politics is not, however, just about constructing new avenues of cooperation. Older development concerns re-emerge in the climate context. Concerns about subsidies to flailing technology sectors whose applications are inappropriate to local Southern contexts for which they were not designed, the use of non-additional tied aid which requires recipients to purchase the technology from the donor have all resurfaced as concerns expressed by developing countries in the climate change debate.[52]

Third, we find that issues of process have been decisive in shaping climate governance outcomes. Who gets to define issues of responsibility, equity, and justice is a function of who participates, who is represented, and who wields most power. Many smaller developing countries have limited representation in the international negotiations, while many more powerful developing countries have moved to bilateral or plurilateral forums where they expect higher returns from their engagement. As climate governance enrolls more actors in complex and disparate ways, questions of accountability come to the fore—whether it is the accountability of CDM project developers to communities expected to host projects, the accountability of bodies such as the Green Climate Fund for the funds it disperses, or compensation for vulnerable areas of the world for climate impacts. This creates enormous challenges for the design of institutions that are transparent and open to participation yet at the same time robust and effective. Indeed, the need to enhance the effectiveness of action across scales and improve the accountability of key actors in climate governance has provided the point of departure for many of the transnational networks that are the subject of the next chapter.

Notes

1 Peter Newell, "Climate for Change: Civil Society and the Politics of Global Warming," in *Global Civil Society Yearbook,* eds Marlies Glasius, Mary Kaldor, and Helmut Anheier (London: Sage, 2005), 90–119; Patrick Bond, *Politics of Climate Justice: Paralysis Above, Movement Below* (Scottsville: University of KwaZulu-Natal Press, 2012).

2 Tom Mitchell and Simon Maxwell, "Defining Climate Compatible Development," *CDKN Policy Brief November* (London: Climate and Development Knowledge Network, 2010).

3 J. Timmons Roberts and Bradley C. Parks, *A Climate of Injustice: Global Inequality, North–South Politics, and Climate Policy* (Cambridge, Mass.: MIT Press, 2007); Chukwumerije Okereke, *Global Justice and Neoliberal Environmental Governance Ethics, Sustainable Development and International Cooperation* (London: Routledge, 2008).

4 Bradley C. Parks and J. Timmons Roberts, "Globalization, Vulnerability to Climate Change and Perceived Injustice," *Society and Natural Resources* 19, no. 4 (2006): 342; Tearfund, *Dried Up, Drowned Out: Voices from the Developing World on a Changing Climate* (London: Tearfund, 2005); Peter Newell, "Race, Class and the Global Politics of Environmental Inequality," *Global Environmental Politics* 5, no. 3 (2005): 70–94.

5 "The Case for Climate Security," Lecture by the Foreign Secretary, the Rt. Hon. Margaret Beckett MP, Royal United Services Institute, May 10, 2007, available online at http://www.rusi.org/events/past/ref:E464343E93D15A/info:public/infoID:E4643430E3E85A/ [accessed January 21, 2015].

6 Quoted in Peter Newell, "Climate Change, Human Rights and Corporate Accountability," in *Climate Change and Human Rights,* ed. Stephen Humphrey (Cambridge: Cambridge University Press, 2009).

7 Heidi Bachram, "Climate Fraud and Carbon Colonialism: The New Trade in Greenhouse Gases," *Capitalism, Nature, Socialism* 15, no. 4 (2004): 5–20.

8 Raúl Estrada-Oyuela, "First Approaches and Unanswered Questions," in *Issues and Options: The Clean Development Mechanism* (New York: UNDP, 1998): 23–9.

9 Jos G.J. Olivier, Greet Janssens-Maenhout, and Jeroen A.H.W. Peters, *Trends in Global CO$_2$ Emissions; 2012 Report* (The Hague/Bilthoven: PBL Netherlands Environmental Assessment Agency, 2012).

10 Roberts and Parks, *A Climate of Injustice: Global Inequality, North–South Politics, and Climate Policy.*

11 Kevin Anderson and Alice Bows, "Beyond 'Dangerous' Climate Change: Emission Scenarios for a New World," *Philosophical Transactions of the Royal Society A* 369, no. 1934 (2011), 20–44.

12 Karen Turner, Max Munday, Stuart McIntyre, and Christa D. Jensen, "Incorporating Jurisdiction Issues into Regional Carbon Accounts Under Production and Consumption Accounting Principles," *Environment and Planning A* 43, no. 3 (2011): 722–41.

13 Sjur Kasa, Anne Therese Gullberg, and Gørild Heggelund, "The Group of 77 in the International Climate Negotiations: Recent Developments and Future Directions," *International Environmental Agreements: Politics, Law and Economics* 8, no. 2 (2008): 113–27.

14 Peter Newell, "The Governance of Energy Finance: The Public, the Private and the Hybrid," *Global Policy* 2, no. 1 (2011): 94–105.

15 Climate Funds Update, *Fast Start Finance*, available online at http://www.climatefundsupdate.org/about-climate-fund/fast-start-finance [accessed January 21, 2015].

16 World Bank, *Carbon Funds and Facilities* (2014), available online at http://go.worldbank.org/51X7CH8VN0 [accessed January 21, 2015].

17 World Resources Institute, *Correcting the World's Greatest Market Failure: Climate Change and Multilateral Development Banks* (2008), available online at http://www.wri.org/publication/correcting-the-worlds-greatest-market-failure [accessed January 21, 2015].

18 Friends of the Earth (US) and Groundwork (South Africa), eds, *World Bank, Climate Change and Energy Financing: Something Old, Something New?* (April 2011), available online at http://www.criticalcollective.org/?publication=world-bank-climate-change-and-energy-financing [accessed January 21, 2015].

19 Ogunlade Davidson, Kirsten Halsnæs, Saleemul Huq, Marcel Kok, Bert Metz, Youba Sokona, and Jan Verhagen, "The Development and Climate Nexus: The Case of Sub-Saharan Africa," *Climate Policy* 3, no.1 (2003): 97–113.

20 UNFCCC, *Investment and Financial Flows to Address Climate Change* (Bonn, Germany: UNFCCC, 2007).

21 UNFCCC, *Investment and Financial Flows to Address Climate Change*, 26.

22 *Report of the Secretary-General's High-level Advisory Group on Climate Change Financing* (New York: UN, November 5, 2010).

23 UNFCCC, *Investment and Financial Flows to Address Climate Change*, Executive summary.

24 Adaptation Fund, *About the Adaptation Fund*, available online at https://www.adaptation-fund.org/about [accessed January 21, 2015].

25 Emily Boyd, Nathan Hultman, Timmons Roberts, Esteve Corbera, Johannes Ebeling, Diana M. Liverman, Kate Brown, Robert Tippmann, John Cole, Phil Mann, Marius Kaiser, Mike Robbins, Adam Bumpus, Allen Shaw, Eduardo Ferreira, Alex Bozmoski, Chris Villiers, and Jonathan Avis, "The Clean Development Mechanism: An Assessment of Current Practice and Future Approaches for Policy," *Tyndall Centre Working Paper* 114, available online at

http://www.tyndall.ac.uk/content/clean-development-mechanism-assessment-current-practice-and-future-approaches-policy [accessed January 21, 2015]; Karen H. Olsen, "The Clean Development Mechanism's Contribution to Sustainable Development: A Review of the Literature," *Climatic Change* 84, no. 1 (2007): 59–73.

26 Peter Newell, "The Politics and Political Economy of the CDM in Argentina," *Environmental Politics* 23, no. 2 (2014): 321–38; Jon Phillips and Peter Newell, "The Governance of Clean Energy in India: the Clean Development Mechanism (CDM) and Domestic Energy Politics," *Energy Policy* 59 (2013): 654–62.

27 *Mapping Carbon Pricing Initiatives: Developments and Prospects* (Washington: World Bank, 2013).

28 Newell, "The Governance of Energy Finance."

29 Peter Newell, Nicky Jenner, and Lucy Baker, "Governing Clean Development: A Framework for Analysis," *The Governance of Clean Development Working Paper Series*, no. 1 (Norwich, UK: UEA, 2009).

30 World Trade Organization, *Activities of the WTO and the Challenge of Climate Change*, available online at http://www.wto.org/english/tratop_e/envir_e/climate_challenge_e.htm [accessed January 21, 2015].

31 World Bank, *International Trade and Climate Change: Economic, Legal and Institutional Perspectives* (Washington, DC: World Bank, 2007).

32 New Economics Foundation, *Collision Course: Free Trade's Free Ride on the Global Climate* (London: New Economics Foundation, 2003).

33 Neil Adger, "Scales of Governance and Environmental Justice for Adaptation and Mitigation of Climate Change," *Journal of International Development* 13, no. 7 (2001): 921–31.

34 World Bank Group, *Poverty and Climate Change: Reducing the Vulnerability of the Poor Through Adaptation* (Washington, DC: World Bank Group, 2003).

35 Parks and Roberts, "Globalization, Vulnerability to Climate Change and Perceived Injustice," 342.

36 Parks and Roberts "Globalization, Vulnerability to Climate Change and Perceived Injustice," 345.

37 Jouni Paavola and Neil Adger, "Justice and Adaptation to Climate Change," *Tyndall Centre Working Paper* 23 (2002).

38 Peter Newell and Adam Bumpus, "The Global Political Ecology of the CDM," *Global Environmental Politics* 12, no. 4 (2012): 49–68.

39 Bachram, "Climate Fraud and Carbon Colonialism: The New Trade in Greenhouse Gases," 10–12.

40 Jutta Kill, "Land Grab in Uganda in Preparation for CDM Sinks Project," *World Rainforest Movement Bulletin* no. 74, September 2003.

41 Patrick Bond, Rehana Dada, and Graham Erion, eds, *Climate Change, Carbon Trading and Civil Society: Negative Returns on South African Investments* (Scottsville: University of KwaZulu-Natal Press, 2009).

42 Adam Bumpus and Diana Liverman, "Accumulation by De-carbonization and the Governance of Carbon Offsets," *Economic Geography* 84, no. 2 (2008): 127–55; James Fairhead, Melissa Leach, and Ian Scoones, "Green Grabbing: A New Appropriation of Nature?," *Journal of Peasant Studies* 39, no. 2 (2012): 285–307.

43 "Sinks Watch," available online at http://www.sinkswatch.org/ [accessed January 21, 2015].
44 Kevin Watkins, Editor of the UNDP Human Development Report, at its launch in Brazil, November 27. Quoted in Larry Elliot and Ashley Seager, "Cut Carbon By Up to Third to Save Poor, UN Tells West," *The Guardian*, November 28, 2007, available online at www.guardian.co.uk/environment/2007/nov/28/climatechange [accessed January 21, 2015].
45 Stephen Humphrey, ed., *Climate Change and Human Rights* (Cambridge: Cambridge University Press, 2009); Peter Newell, "Civil Society, Corporate Accountability and the Politics of Climate Change," *Global Environmental Politics* 8, no. 3 (2008): 124–55.
46 Earthjustice, "Petition to the Inter-American Commission on Human Rights Seeking Relief From Violations Resulting From Global Warming Caused By Acts and Omissions of the United States," available online at http://earthjustice.org/news/press/2005/inuit-human-rights-petition-filed-over-climate-change [accessed January 21, 2015].
47 Earthjustice, ibid.
48 "Corporate Watch," (2007), available online at http://www.corpwatch.org/article.php?id=979 [accessed January 21, 2015]..
49 Clare Saunders, "The Stop Climate Chaos Coalition: Climate Change as a Development Issue," *Third World Quarterly* 29, no. 8 (2008): 1509–26.
50 New Economics Foundation, *Collision Course*.
51 Robert O. Keohane and David G. Victor, "The Regime Complex for Climate Change," *Discussion paper* 10–33 (Cambridge, Mass.: Harvard Project on International Climate Agreements, 2010).
52 Oliver Tickell and Nicola Hildyard, "Green Dollars, Green Menace," *The Ecologist* 22, no. 3 (1992): 82–3.

3

BETWEEN GLOBAL AND LOCAL

Governing climate change transnationally

As we outline in the Introduction, climate change is an issue of concern not only on international and national agendas (Chapters 1 and 2), but also for an array of transnational networks.[1] A growing number of arrangements which cross national boundaries are being formed by a range of actors with the specific purpose of addressing climate change.[2] In this chapter we explore this transnational phenomenon. First, we examine the roots of transnational climate change governance and the governance "functions" that such networks perform. Second, we consider different types of transnational climate change governance networks—those based purely on the involvement of public actors, those that involve a hybrid of public and private actors, and those that involve only private actors. In the final section, we consider the issues and challenges for governing climate change that this phenomenon raises.

Transnational networks and climate change

Transnational relations are not new. In the early 1970s, Keohane and Nye were among the first to draw attention to the significance of these cross-border transactions and networks, which seemingly bypassed the central organization and control of national governments.[3] As the debate on global governance (see Introduction) gathered pace during the 1990s, a range of scholars pointed to the importance of transnational coalitions and networks in influencing the development of policy in various spheres of global affairs and in undertaking governance in their own right.[4] The presence of arrangements that sought to govern global environmental issues outside of the remit of international regimes and without the necessary involvement of nation-states provided one of the foundations for the argument that a different way of approaching global politics was required.

The emergence of transnational climate change governance

In the climate change arena, the presence of such networks can be traced back to the beginning of social and political concern for the issue. For example, transnational networks of municipal governments such as the Climate Alliance and ICLEI's[5] Cities for Climate Protection (CCP) originated in the early 1990s as both climate change and sustainability began to become significant issues for local authorities. However, most transnational arrangements are more recent, post-dating the 1997 Kyoto Protocol, and in the ensuing decade their numbers and profile have increased significantly.[6] Why might this be the case? Karin Bäckstrand suggests that the recent growth of transnational arrangements can be seen as a "response to the regulatory deficit or implementation deficit permeating multilateral regimes."[7] In other words, the emergence of transnational governance could be regarded as a response to the perceived failures and limitations of more traditional international institutions and national governments in addressing the problem of climate change, some of which we have discussed in Chapters 1 and 2. Taking a slightly different line of argument, Andonova *et al.* point to the specific characteristics of the climate change issue as providing fertile ground for the emergence of transnational governance networks.[8] First, the diversity of national commitments in the international climate regime creates opportunities for alternative forms of cooperation between actors subject to international targets and those who are not. Second, the inclusion of flexible mechanisms in the Kyoto Protocol has led to the involvement of a range of new actors working across borders in the design and implementation of international climate policy. We saw in Chapters 1 and 2 how, despite being market mechanisms, they still involve high levels of state involvement and require a range of governance functions to be performed by project developers, mediators, and verifiers. Third, the complexity and breadth of climate change as a policy agenda offers potential for issue- and sector-specific collaborations alongside international agreements. In short, the nature of the climate change governance problem and how it is being addressed has created the political space for new collaborations and mechanisms of governance, such as the transnational initiatives that are our focus in this chapter.

However, it is important to realize that the emergence of transnational climate change governance has not taken place in a political, social, or economic vacuum. As we have seen in Chapters 1 and 2, broader trends— frequently referred to by terms such as globalization and neo-liberalism— have provided both the means and the rationale for the involvement of multiple actors in seeking to shape the governance of a range of local to global problems. Across many nation-states, principles of neo-liberalism have been used as the basis for reducing the role of the state and increasing the role of the private sector in service delivery. Various forms of partnership have been promoted as the means through which to determine public policy goals and deliver governance. In the environmental arena, the argument that responsibilities for governing global issues should be shared between public and private actors was epitomized by the 2002 World Summit on Sustainable Development (WSSD) which established the role of so-called Type II partnerships (between public and private actors) in delivering sustainability.[9] This is a role that many non-state actors have actively sought, on the basis of arguments about their relative expertise, ability to engage with a range of different communities, and for reasons of corporate social responsibility (see Chapters 4 and 5). We suggest that it is this context, together with the specific characteristics of climate change as a governance problem, which has led to the emergence of transnational climate change governance.[10]

Governing transnationally

Having recognized that transnational networks now form an important part of the governance landscape for climate change, the critical questions that emerge are whether, how, and why such networks are able to have any effect. While international regimes and national governments can deploy binding agreements and various policy instruments, such as economic incentives or sanctions, transnational networks do not on face value seem to have much at their disposal in terms of the standard means of shaping behavior or ensuring compliance with particular targets, goals, and norms. However, the range of mechanisms and instruments that networks deploy include measures which are traditionally seen as "soft," such as information-sharing or capacity building and implementation, as well as those which imply a degree of enforcement and rule-setting, such as those that accompany funding, certification, or mandatory requirements for membership of any one transnational organization.[11] These three broad categories of governance functions are not mutually exclusive—some transnational networks may use a combination of information-sharing, capacity building, and rule-setting approaches, while others may focus on one particular function (see Box 3.1). Analysis suggests that "few initiatives undertake *only* information-sharing or capacity building (13 percent); most have some form of target, monitoring or rule-setting function (75 percent)."[12]

BOX 3.1 EXAMPLES OF TRANSNATIONAL GOVERNANCE

Information-sharing

The Climate Group aims to "convene leaders, share hard evidence of successful low carbon growth, and pilot practical solutions which can be replicated worldwide."

Source: The Climate Group, *About Us*, http://www.theclimategroup.org/who-we-are/about-us/ [accessed November 2014].

Implementation and capacity building

The Renewable Energy and Energy Efficiency Partnership (REEEP) "invests in clean energy markets to help developing countries expand modern energy services and improve lives; increase prosperity and economic dynamism; and keep CO_2 emissions in check: a paradigm commonly known as green growth. REEEP's tools are modern clean energy technologies – renewable energy and energy efficiency – market forces, and knowledge management."

Source: http://www.reeep.org/services [accessed November 2014].

Regulation

The Regional Greenhouse Gas Initiative (RGGI) states that "the RGGI states implemented a new 2014 RGGI cap of 91 million short tons. The RGGI CO_2 cap then declines 2.5 percent each year from 2015 to 2020. The RGGI CO_2 cap represents a regional budget for CO_2 emissions from the power sector."

Source: RGGI, *Welcome*, http://www.rggi.org/ [accessed November 2014].

Within transnational networks, information-sharing can perform crucial governance functions by framing issues, setting agendas, defining what counts as responsible or effective action, offering inspiration, and providing a means of benchmarking achievements. In the context of transnational governance, information-sharing is usually orientated towards network constituents and acts both to reinforce engagement and to police its boundaries. A second set of governance functions relating to implementation and capacity building is regarded as particularly important in those transnational networks which have emerged as a result of the 2002 WSSD and other multilateral environmental agreements.[13] Through the provision of resources, transnational networks seek to develop the capacity of their constituents to act on climate change by providing access to expertise, funding, or technologies that would otherwise be unavailable. In some cases, transnational networks are seeking to develop the capacity to implement or respond to international or national policy frameworks, such as contributing to meeting targets set in the Kyoto Protocol or being able to participate in the CDM. In other cases, transnational arrangements are seeking to build capacity in response to network aims and goals. A third set of governance functions that transnational networks undertake involves regulation. This can take place through setting particular standards, such as goals for emission reductions or certification schemes, establishing a particular basis for membership, for example, signing up to a specific program of actions or a code of conduct, or various means of measuring performance. Networks vary considerably in the extent to which they use and implement regulations. However, despite the supposedly voluntary nature of transnational climate change governance, the presence of regulation and (sometimes) sanctions suggest that networks are able to exert a degree of power over their members.

In the absence of the traditional governance toolkits of nation-states and international institutions, transnational governance arrangements have devised a range of means through which they seek to guide and direct their constituents towards particular goals. At one end of the spectrum, practices of sharing information could be regarded as entirely voluntary, yet in the process of establishing what does and does not count as best practice, for example, transnational arrangements can exert considerable pressure on members to conform to particular ways of working or to certain norms. Once one or two key market players participate in a scheme like the Carbon Disclosure Project (CDP) (see Chapter 4), there is peer pressure on others to show investors that they are willing to report on their emissions profile. Sharing information in this manner can serve to define the agenda, and determine how the climate change problem should be tackled. Means of building capacity could equally be regarded as voluntary—members are free to join in with project proposals, to take or leave advice, or to disregard funding opportunities. Again, however, by being able to determine the criteria upon which funding is distributed, to set the rules of the game, and by providing certain forms of advice or access to particular sorts of technologies or information, networks can also find themselves in powerful positions with respect to their constituents. Transnational networks also undertake explicit forms of regulation, establishing standards and disclosing performance, developing membership rules, and, on occasion, sanctioning those who fail to comply. Despite their apparently voluntary nature and weak position, through these means transnational networks are able to govern by shaping the ideas and behavior of their constituents in accordance with certain norms and goals for addressing climate change, suggesting that they warrant further exploration as part of the contemporary landscape of climate governance.

Comparing types of transnational climate change governance

Transnational climate change governance arrangements involve a whole host of actors—from municipal governments to private foundations, non-governmental organizations to multinational corporations. These networks take on different characteristics depending on whether they are constituted by public actors (e.g. subnational governments), private actors (e.g. corporations), or a hybrid of public and private actors. Here, we outline the different types of transnational network involved in governing climate change and compare their roles with respect to the functions of information-sharing, implementation and capacity building, and regulation discussed above.

Governing beyond but through the state: public transnational governance

Transnational environmental governance may involve networks of public actors including, for example, sub-units of central government, regional or state authorities, and city or local governments. In the climate domain, examples include transnational municipal networks, discussed in more detail below, networks of regional governments, such as the New England Governors and the Eastern Canadian Premiers (NEG-ECP) 2001 initiative to adopt a joint Climate Change Action Plan[14] and the Network of Regional Governments for Sustainable Development (nrg4SD), as well as bilateral agreements between subnational governments to act on climate change, such as the initiative between California (United States) and Victoria (Australia).

Municipal networks provide one of the first and most extensive examples of transnational governance. In the early 1990s, three transnational municipal networks—Climate Alliance, ICLEI CCP, and Energy Cities—were established with member cities in Europe and the United States.[15] Founded in 1990 as an alliance between European cities and indigenous peoples, Climate Alliance has over 1,600 members in 20 European countries with a concentration in Germany, Austria, and the Netherlands.[16] Its aim is to reduce emissions to 50 percent below 1990 by 2030 and protect the rainforest through partnerships and projects with indigenous rainforest peoples.[17] Cities for Climate Protection was formed in 1992 as an initiative of ICLEI.[18] Municipal membership of the CCP network initially reflected its origins in North America and Europe, but by 2009 had expanded with specific campaigns in Australia, Canada, Europe, Latin America, Mexico, New Zealand, South Africa, South Asia, Southeast Asia, and the United States, and over 1,000 members worldwide.[19] Members of CCP pledged to reduce their emissions of GHG by between 10 and 20 percent from 1990 levels by 2010. Energy Cities stemmed from a project funded by the Commission of the European Union and is a somewhat different network, with an explicit focus on local energy policy in which addressing climate change is but one factor. Founded in 1990 and based in France, it now has over 200 individual members in 21 European countries and represents over 1,000 municipalities.[20] While its members are primarily municipalities, the network also includes local energy management agencies, municipal companies, and groups of municipalities. In this way, its reach may be greater than its membership numbers suggest.[21]

In the mid-2000s, just as membership and interest in these initial networks appeared to be stagnating, a new wave of transnational municipal networks emerged and the work of existing networks was reinvigorated. Following the success of the 2005 US Mayors' Climate Protection Agreement,[22] in which cities pledged to meet or beat the Kyoto Protocol targets in their own communities, ICLEI has supported the development of the World Mayors' Council on Climate Change with the explicit purpose "to politically promote climate protection policies at the local level."[23] In 2008, the EU Covenant of Mayors was formed with the aim of contributing to the goal of meeting and exceeding the EU policy goal of reducing carbon dioxide emissions by 20 percent by 2020. With over 5,800 members, it is now the largest municipal movement seeking to address climate change.[24] Smaller in scale but critical in economic and political terms, the emergence of the C40 Climate Leadership Group (C40) also signals the more avowedly political nature of this second wave of transnational municipal networks. This network was instigated by the Mayor of London and The Climate Group (TCG) and formed by 18 cities in 2005 as a parallel initiative to the Group of Eight (G8) Gleneagles summit on climate change. In 2007, this network entered into a partnership with the

Clinton Climate Initiative (CCI) and expanded its membership to include 40 of the largest cities in the world, and the organizations were formally aligned into a closer collaboration in 2011.[25] Activities within the network have included collaboration with Microsoft to produce software for GHG emissions accounting at the city scale, and the Energy Efficiency Building Retrofit Program, which brings together "public and private organizations, including governments, the financial community and other non-profits to highlight, design, and test innovative solutions to financing, contracting, and procurement, with the goal of developing and scaling these models nationally."[26] While ostensibly a network of municipal governments, the central involvement of both the Clinton Foundation and TCG in its founding stages indicate that, in practice, the boundaries between public and private actors in transnational climate governance are increasingly blurred. Reflecting this evolving landscape, in 2012 at the Rio+20 Summit ICLEI launched Green Climate Cities to replace their long running Cities for Climate Protection program and integrate a number of the tools and initiatives they have developed over the past decade, including a global protocol for GHG emissions reporting and the database on climate action, carbon*n* Cities Climate Registry (cCR).[27]

These new developments have both served to create an ever more interlinked landscape of urban responses to climate change and helped to raise the profile of municipal leadership internationally. At COP 13 in Bali in 2008, municipalities formed the second largest delegation and signed the Bali World Mayors and Local Governments Climate Protection Agreement to tackle both mitigation and adaptation. The growing momentum behind urban responses led the World Bank in 2010[28] and UN-Habitat in 2011[29] to publish special reports on the critical need to understand and develop urban responses to climate change. In 2014, the UN Secretary-General called a summit of business and city leaders in New York to highlight the importance of an urban response to climate change, further cementing the central role now seen for municipal authorities in the international politics of climate change.

Across these various transnational municipal networks, it is possible to find evidence of information-sharing, implementation and capacity building, as well as rule-setting. Information-sharing functions

> are the bread and butter of [transnational municipal networks]. Networks are frequently established for the explicit purpose of creating and sharing "best" or "good" practice, and municipalities indicate that the opportunity to learn about "what works" from other places is a key motivation for their participation.[30]

For example, transnational municipal networks frequently collate examples of best practice in databases, disseminate case studies through newsletters, or may even, as is the case with Energy Cities, organize study tours where groups of local officials and politicians seek to learn at firsthand how local energy policies were created.[31] Municipal networks also undertake various forms of audit and inventories of municipal GHG emissions and action plans which are made available to other members. Such strategies have the advantage of being open and inclusive, as well as avoiding the need for explicit forms of intervention or the use of more hierarchical forms of authority within the network. However, their success as governance strategies is open to debate. There is little evidence, for example, that the recognition and dissemination of best practice leads to action in a direct sense[32] or that improved knowledge of local emissions necessarily leads to policy implementation.[33] Rather, these sorts of information-sharing activities are often most effective in terms of framing a policy problem, in order to persuade others about the need for, and possibilities of, action. By framing the nature of the climate policy problem and its appropriate solutions, strategies of information-sharing both serve to delimit the field of action and offer a means of monitoring performance amongst network members,[34] in turn making the problem of climate change governable at the municipal level.

Transnational municipal networks are also involved in governance through implementation and capacity building. Given that municipalities are not directly charged with implementing international environmental agreements, such as the Kyoto Protocol, such activities are primarily orientated towards achieving national or local policy objectives, as well as meeting the goals established by the network. In the European context, one mechanism through which this strategy has been pursued is through securing funding for particular projects. For example, the Climate Alliance is funded for the coordination and evaluation of the European Mobility Week.[35] Securing additional, external funding is also important for other municipal networks. One of the key features of the C40 network has been its partnership with the CCI and the leverage of funding for a program of energy efficiency improvements in office buildings. Transnational municipal networks are also able to access national funding, either to set funds aside specifically for the program, as was the case with CCP Australia,[36] or by working with members to access existing funding programs.

The regulative functions of transnational municipal networks are particularly interesting, given the public actors involved in these networks and the traditional association between regulation and forms of public authority.

Several different forms of standard and rule setting are apparent. The first relates to forms of recognition, in which meeting particular standards of performance are explicitly rewarded by the network. One such example is the "Climate Star," awarded annually by the Climate Alliance to municipalities for their achievements.[37] A second regulative strategy employed by transnational networks has been that of benchmarking. The CCP network was based around a series of five milestones of progress, involving conducting an emissions inventory, setting an emissions reduction target, formulating an action plan, implementing policies, and monitoring progress, and the most recent developments in this field by the CCP parent organization, ICLEI, involve working on the development of a global protocol for emissions reporting and the carbon*n* registry of urban climate initiatives that focuses on measurement and verification.[38] Rather than being based on hard rules, the regulative function of climate governance within municipal networks is more akin to processes of voluntary standard setting, where compliance is achieved both as a result of the recognition on the part of the municipality of the authority of the network and through processes of peer pressure and competition.

Towards partnership? Hybrid transnational governance

A second type of transnational climate change governance, termed hybrid, involves actors from the public and private spheres in various forms of collaboration. Central to the emergence of hybrid transnational governance has been the growing emphasis in multilateral forums, international organizations, and national governments, as well as amongst some sections of the business and NGO communities, on public–private partnerships (PPP) as a means of effecting global governance.[39] The WSSD held in Johannesburg in 2002 promoted the use of these so-called Type II agreements as a means of pursuing sustainable development alongside formal international (Type I) agreements. Bäckstrand defines PPP as "institutionalized cooperative relationships between public actors (governments and intergovernmental organizations) and private actors (corporate and civil society actors)."[40] These formalized PPP are an important feature of the transnational climate change governance landscape. However, in the context of growing neoliberal orthodoxies about the role of the state and other actors, more informal hybrid arrangements have also emerged through the collaboration of public and private actors as a means of governing climate change.

Turning first to formalized PPP, of the 334 Johannesburg Type II agreements, approximately 90 are concerned with issues of energy and climate change, though perhaps only 34 are explicitly directed to the issue of climate change.[41] One of the largest and most complex is REEEP. Formed on the initiative of the UK government in the immediate aftermath of the WSSD, REEEP is organized through an international office and four regional secretariats. Its membership comprises national and subnational governments, international organizations, businesses, and NGOs, and "in the ten years since its inception, the organization has grown to comprise 385 Partner organizations including 45 governments as well as a range of private companies and international organizations."[42] Its mission is "to accelerate the global market for sustainable energy with a primary focus on developing countries and emerging markets."[43] In terms of its governance functions, REEEP engages both with information-sharing and implementation and capacity building. The regionalized structure of REEEP is intended to capture existing knowledge about the barriers and opportunities for enhancing renewable energy and energy efficiency, and secretariats undertake various dissemination activities and events. At the same time, drawing on funding from various national governments, REEEP is involved in the selection and support of projects to develop new technologies and markets for renewables and energy efficiency. While such projects may assist in helping countries to meet their commitments under international frameworks for climate change (i.e. the UNFCCC and Kyoto Protocol), the focus here is more on developing capacity in the energy sector more broadly, especially with regard to changing the regulatory and market conditions for the implementation of energy efficiency and renewable energy technologies in developing economies.

Another arena within which formal PPP have been created is in the implementation of one of the Kyoto flexible mechanisms, the CDM (see Chapter 1). While the formation and regulation of the CDM process takes place within the international arena, Bäckstrand[44] suggests that CDM projects, of which more than 7,500 are now registered,[45] can be regarded as public–private partnerships because of the range of actors, including host governments, private investors, carbon brokers, and NGOs involved in their design, implementation, and verification. Streck, for instance, describes the CDM as "an innovative model of cooperation between the private and public sectors."[46] The collaborative network structure in which state and non-state actors collaborate in a partnership arrangement confers on non-state actors, such as the approved auditing bodies known as Designated Operational Entities, "a variety of voluntary, self-formal and formal roles in formulating policy responses and implementing international agreements."[47] However, as we discuss in more detail in Chapters 4 and 5, the ways in which such forms of governance operate in practice is highly disputed, demonstrating that the function of implementation cannot be understood just as a means through which internationally agreed goals are transmitted to particular places, but rather is a means through which what constitutes just and appropriate responses to climate change are constructed and contested. In this light, each of the actors involved in the CDM project cycle have a significant role in determining what counts as a reduction in GHG and the extent to which sustainable development benefits are realized. Because it operates as a market mechanism, credits in the form of Certified Emission Reductions (CERs) are issued for reductions in GHG that (in theory) would not have otherwise been possible, but no monetary value is attached to sustainable development benefits. This explains why investors have prioritized projects which earn them most CERs without necessarily delivering the greatest benefits to communities that host the projects.[48] The CDM highlights the intertwined nature of the international regime and transnational governance. While ostensibly created by and for nation-states, the UNFCCC and the Kyoto Protocol are increasingly reliant on the emergence of transnational hybrid networks for their implementation.[49]

As well as being driven through multilateral processes, hybrid transnational governance has also emerged from the bottom up. One such example is TCG, a UK-based network. Launched in 2004 by then Prime Minister Tony Blair, TCG was initiated by the Rockefeller Brothers Foundation as a means of fostering dialogue between those corporations and subnational governments in the United States who were taking a progressive approach to addressing climate change and their European counterparts. Membership is on a fee-paying basis and now includes over 100 members from businesses, state, regional, and city governments, organized through a European headquarters based in the United Kingdom and regional offices in the United States, India, and China. TCG has undertaken a range of information-sharing activities, including the production and promotion of examples of best practice, publicity events about the significance of climate change and forms of peer-to-peer learning. In addition, the network has been involved with various projects aimed at implementation and capacity building including the States and Regions Initiative whose members are "phasing out coal, committing to 100 percent renewables, investing in clean tech infrastructure and start-ups, linking emissions trading systems, developing new financing mechanisms and making ambitious emissions reductions commitments"[50] as well as regulative functions through the development and promotion of the Voluntary Carbon Standard (VCS) (see Chapter 4).[51] The complexity and range of the different forms of governance taking place within TCG, as well as formal partnerships such as REEEP and the implementation of international policy instruments such as the CDM, suggest that such initiatives go beyond the sorts of organizational structures of non-governmental and business coalitions that characterized the landscape of climate governance in the 1990s. Instead, such initiatives are forging what John Ruggie terms a "new global public domain," "an increasingly institutionalized transnational arena of discourse, contestation, and action concerning the production of global public goods, involving private as well as public actors."[52] The emergence of this transnational domain of climate change governance raises significant issues in terms of legitimacy and effectiveness, to which we return below.

Self-regulation and private transnational governance

Alongside hybrid and public forms of transnational governance, private initiatives and networks are also contributing to the emergence of the "new global public domain."[53] Scholars have documented private transnational governance in a number of fields including forestry, water, chemicals, and food.[54] Private transnational governance involves a variety of non-state actors, including corporate and civil society sectors, in arrangements through which "issues are defined, rules are made, and compliance with these rules is monitored"[55] beyond the direct purview of nation-states or other actors from the public sphere.

One means by which private transnational governance has emerged with respect to climate change is through the work of business leadership groups, orchestrated by bodies such as the World Business Council on Sustainable Development (WBCSD) or "think tanks" such as the World Resources Institute (WRI). One initiative that was established by the WBCSD and led by the Swedish energy company Vattenfall between 2008 and 2012 was Combat Climate Change (3C). It aimed to establish a global opinion group on the need for international action on climate change, and in so doing asked its members to commit to a series of principles about the nature of the climate change problem and how it should be governed, in effect leading to the development of norms concerning climate change governance in the private transnational arena. Another example is the "Mind the Science, Mind the Gap" project launched by WRI, CDP, and WWF in 2014, which aims to "develop a new, sector-specific methodology that helps companies set science-based emission-reduction targets based on the IPCC decarbonization pathway that would keep global temperature rise below 2 °C."[56]

A second means through which private transnational governance networks are being forged is through partnership working between corporate and civil society actors. The Climate Community and Biodiversity Alliance (CCBA) was founded in 2003 by Conservation International, and includes corporations such as BP and Intel as well as other NGOs, such as Rainforest Alliance and The Nature Conservancy Council.[57] The CCBA has established the CCB standard for land management projects that simultaneously address climate change, social goals, and biodiversity conservation. Since the standards were released in 2005, over 80 projects have been given validation.[58] As well as performing a regulative function through the promotion of voluntary standards for land management, the CCB also serves an implementation and capacity building function through enabling action on elements of international climate policy, including the CDM and Reducing Emissions from Deforestation and forest Degradation (REDD). The promotion of standards for carbon offset markets has been another key area in which private governance initiatives have flourished (see Chapter 4). The predominance of private forms of transnational governance that focus on certification and monitoring has led to the finding that, in relation to public and hybrid forms, "private actors more often use rule setting, monitoring and certification compared to other initiatives" yet the continued dominance of "soft" measures, based on information-sharing and capacity, mean that "a majority [of private initiatives] are not able or willing to commit themselves to ambitious or difficult actions" in order to pursue the transnational governance of climate change.[59]

Alongside the growth in hybrid forms of transnational governance, it is perhaps the growing involvement of private actors in governing what many perceive as a fundamentally public issue—the global climate—that has raised the most concerns. On the one hand, critics have argued that the increasing involvement of non-state actors and, in particular, private sector organizations, in climate governance is detrimental in terms of the legitimacy of, and accountability for, decision making. This is either seen as a form of "greenwash," where corporate actors in particular seek to avoid or deflect attention away from more serious forms of action, or as part of a broader trend towards the privatization of governance in which private actors come to dominate public governance institutions and assume more "government-like" functions themselves.[60] On the other hand, commentators have also pointed to the highly fragmented and limited nature of transnational governance arrangements—despite the growing numbers of municipalities, regions, businesses, and NGOs involved, the vast majority remain outside of this "new global public domain."[61] While transnational climate change governance may be interesting in principle, to date its capacity to make a difference in terms of reducing emissions of GHG may seem limited.

Governance issues and challenges

Transnational initiatives for addressing climate change are now firmly established on the governance landscape. Their presence signifies the broad and growing constituency for whom climate change is an issue of importance, and may be read as opening up the climate change domain to a wider variety of actors and to different perspectives on addressing the problem. However, the emergence of transnational climate change governance also raises a number of challenges.

First, we can see from this chapter that in terms of the impact and effectiveness of transnational climate governance, tracing the links between particular initiatives and progress either in terms of absolute reductions of emissions or in developing momentum behind climate policy is a challenge. As researchers have also found in relation to the international regime, the causal chains between policies, interventions, actions, and outcomes are complex and multiple, such that definitive conclusions are hard to reach. Furthermore, given the short timescales over which they have been operating, the lack of common baselines, and the multiple measures used to record reductions of GHG emissions, assessing the difference that such initiatives are collectively making in terms of addressing climate change is almost impossible. However, there are some ways in which their effectiveness can be gauged and there is some evidence from particular initiatives that impacts are being achieved. For example, ICLEI Australia suggest that the CCP program resulted in a saving of 4.7 million tons of carbon dioxide equivalent in 2007/8, and a total of 18 million tons since the program started in Australia in 1998/9.[62]

Second, many networks and partnerships include targets and timetables for reducing emissions of GHG that go far beyond those agreed internationally. This may create momentum for action towards these ambitious goals and ease the path of any future international agreements.[63] Further, some analysts suggest that the continued work and effectiveness of the international regime is bound up with the transnational governing of climate change.[64] As the IPCC note:

> the landscape of international institutions related to climate policy has become significantly more complex. Climate change is addressed in a growing number of fora and institutions and across a wider range of scales [such that] careful design of linkages and cooperative arrangements will be needed to manage the increasingly fragmented regime complex to prevent conflicts among institutions . . . avoid gaps or loopholes . . . and maximize potential institutional synergies.[65]

Third, many such initiatives target emissions of GHG that are not covered by international and national climate policy, which has tended to focus on emission reductions from the energy and industrial sectors. For example, initiatives such as C40 focus on energy consumption in the commercial building sector, while others concerned with regulating carbon offsets address the climate impacts of individual consumption. This suggests that the effectiveness and impact of transnational climate governance will not only be realized in the traditional arenas of climate policy, but may also be more effective if, where, and when it is able to foster action at the local, regional, and national levels through the development of initiatives that have co-benefits beyond the climate change domain. Nonetheless, a key challenge here is the additionality of these initiatives—are they mobilizing action that would otherwise not have taken place, or acting as window dressing for actions already underway? Either way, there is certainly no evidence that such initiatives are any worse than international agreements in terms of their impacts and effectiveness, and they may—by achieving modest emission reductions, creating "coalitions of the willing," and raising expectations about what it is possible to achieve—be acting in a way that is complementary to the international regime. If, however, such initiatives were to act as a distraction from international agreements, or a substitute for them, the outcomes in terms of the effect on addressing climate change might be much less benign.

We have also seen that transnational climate governance initiatives raise significant challenges in terms of accountability. Once the governing of climate change moves from discernible public arenas of government, questions concerning who is participating, on whose behalf, and how they are held to account, are inevitably raised. Conceiving of accountability as involving both answerability—the need to justify and explain positions and actions adopted—and enforceability—the ability to impose sanction for non-compliance—can help to examine the complex questions raised by transnational climate governance.[66] On the one hand, such initiatives may have done much to promote the answerability of a range of actors in terms of their actions on climate change. One feature of many of the partnerships and networks discussed in this chapter is their focus on making their actions accountable through mechanisms such as audit, disclosure, peer review, standard setting, and other forms of soft regulation. In this way, they may serve to increase the accountability of various actors to new constituencies concerned with climate change. On the other hand, it is clear that the ability of such initiatives to enforce standards and to implement particular actions is limited. In the absence of forms of sanction, network members or constituencies may have little recourse should action not be forthcoming. In this manner, transnational climate governance has much in common with the international regime, which has not only raised the issue of the answerability of nation-states for addressing climate change, but also demonstrated its weakness in enforcing the targets and timetables agreed.

One of the consequences of the partial accountability of transnational climate governance is that, unlike the international negotiating forums and national policy contexts discussed in Chapter 2, issues of equity are rarely visited. Issues of procedural equity—who is able to participate in such initiatives—and distributive equity—what the impacts of such initiatives might be in terms of social and environmental justice—are critical. Turning to the equity of participation, it is clear that initiatives vary significantly in terms of their inclusivity and the sharing of the benefits of network participation. Some, such as CCP and Climate Alliance for example, are ostensibly open, seeking to recruit as many members as possible. Others are based on an exclusivity of membership, for either geographic or strategic reasons. However, even in the case of open initiatives, there are significant barriers to involvement, including the capacity required to set up membership and to access funding, as well as the way in which the problem of climate change governance has been framed which has to date mainly been in accordance with Northern concerns for mitigation and energy efficiency, rather than, say, issues of adaptation and the provision of basic services, though this picture is now changing. In terms of the equity of impact, there has to date been little analysis of the implications of transnational initiatives in terms of issues of social and environmental justice. As we discuss in more depth in Chapters 1, 2, and 4, CDM projects have been found to have mixed benefits for the communities in which they are based, and it is likely that projects carried out under the auspices of other forms of transnational governance may have similar impacts. At the same time, given the partial nature of involvement in such initiatives, attempts to govern climate change in one location or firm may serve to push "dirty" industries outside these jurisdictions, with negative consequences for other communities without the power to resist them. Such impacts are, of course, not unique to transnational forms of climate governance, but do suggest that their wider implications for sustainable development and socio-environmental justice need to be considered in their development and implementation.

Overall, we find that transnational climate change governance raises significant issues in terms of effectiveness, accountability, and equity. In part, these challenges arise because such initiatives transcend and cut across the frameworks through which we have traditionally analyzed the politics of global affairs. Consequently, there are three ways in which the phenomenon of transnational governance requires us to reconsider the notion of global governance. First, in relation to the spatial organization of global politics. Rather than taking place within discrete and hierarchically arranged levels of governance, the transnational governance phenomenon is complex, where so-called local initiatives may have a reach across national jurisdictions, and international agreements give rise to new forms of regional or local partnerships. This finding reinforces our conclusions in Chapter 1 that tracing the location of climate governance is no longer straightforward. Second, with respect to the relationship between state and non-state actors, transnational governance initiatives raise questions as to whether these demarcations are analytically useful, given their hybridity, the mixing of roles, and the extension of forms of public authority into ostensibly private domains and vice versa. As we saw in Chapter 2, the increasing crossover between policy issues and between institutions, and the proliferation of actors involved in climate governance, calls into question where the boundaries between the public and the private might lie. Finally, transnational governance initiatives demonstrate not only the importance of the power of one set of actors over another, as currently captured in many analyses of international relations, but also in a more dynamic sense, where power is exercised in the framing of the climate problem, and in the day-to-day activities of networks and partnerships where power-sharing and agreed norms of conduct are key to their success. Conceiving of climate governance as taking place outside of the international regime in transnational initiatives, therefore, raises some fundamental questions about how, where, and why the governing of global affairs takes place, issues to which we return in the Conclusion.

Notes

1 Throughout the chapter, the terms "network" and "arrangement" are used interchangeably to describe transnational collaboration between various types of actor. Not all of these phenomena could be classified as "networks" in organizational terms, and nor should the term imply that power relations amongst those participating are necessarily absent or that each is equally active or vital to the network.

2 Harriet Bulkeley, Liliana Andonva, Michele M. Betsill, Daniel Compagnon, Thomas Hale, Peter Newell, Matthew Paterson, Charlie Rogers, and Stacy Vanderveer, *Transnational Climate Change Governance* (New York: Cambridge University Press, 2014).

3 Robert Keohane and Joseph Nye, *Transnational Relations and World Politics* (Cambridge, Mass.: Harvard University Press, 1971).

4 Liliana Andonova and Marc Levy, "Franchising Global Governance: Making Sense of the Johannesburg Type II Partnerships," in *Yearbook of*

International Cooperation on Environment and Development 2003/2004 (London: Earthscan Publications, 2003); Ben Cashore, Graeme Auld, and Deanna Newsom, *Governing through Markets: Forest Certification and the Emergence of Non-State Authority* (New Haven, Conn.: Yale University Press, 2004); Jennifer Clapp, "The Privatisation of Global Environmental Governance: ISO 14001 and the Developing World," *Global Governance* 4, no. 3 (1998): 295–316; Pieter Glasbergen, Frank Biermann, and Arthur P. J. Mol, *Partnerships, Governance and Sustainable Development: Reflections on Theory and Practice* (Cheltenham, UK: Edward Elgar, 2007); Peter M. Haas, "Do Regimes Matter? Epistemic Committees and Mediterranean Pollution Control," *International Organization* 43, no. 3 (1989): 377–403; Margaret E. Keck and Kathryn Sikkink, *Activists Beyond Borders. Advocacy Networks in International Politics* (Ithaca, NY: Cornell University Press, 1998); Ann-Marie Slaughter, *A New World Order* (Princeton, NJ: Princeton University Press, 2004).

5 Once known as the International Council for Local Environmental Initiatives, ICLEI now goes by its acronym and the title Local Governments for Sustainability.

6 Bulkeley *et al.*, *Transnational Climate Change Governance*.

7 Karin Bäckstrand, "Accountability of Networked Climate Governance: The Rise of Transnational Climate Partnerships," *Global Environmental Politics* 8, no. 3 (2008): 75.

8 Liliana Andonova, Michele M. Betsill, and Harriet Bulkeley, "Transnational Climate Governance," *Global Environmental Politics* 9, no. 2 (2009): 52–73.

9 Liliana B. Andonova, Michele M. Betsill, and Harriet Bulkeley, "Transnational Climate Governance"; Philipp Pattberg and Johannes Stripple, "Beyond the Public and Private Divide: Remapping Transnational Climate Governance in the 21st Century," *International Environmental Agreements: Politics, Law and Economics* 8, no. 4 (2008): 367–88.

10 Matthew J. Hoffmann, *Climate Governance at the Crossroads: Experimenting with a Global Response after Kyoto* (Oxford: Oxford University Press, 2011).

11 Andonova *et al.*, "Transnational Climate Governance"; Bulkeley *et al.*, *Transnational Climate Change Governance*.

12 Bulkeley *et al.*, *Transnational Climate Change Governance*, 604.

13 Thorsten Benner, Wolfgang Reinicke, and Jan Witte, "Multisectoral Networks in Global Governance: Towards a Pluralistic System of Accountability," *Government and Opposition* 39, no. 2 (2004): 191–210.

14 Henrik Selin and Stacy VanDeveer, "Canadian–U.S. Environmental Cooperation: Climate Change Networks and Regional Action," *American Review of Canadian Studies* (Summer 2005): 253–78.

15 Harriet Bulkeley and Michele M. Betsill, *Cities and Climate Change: Urban Sustainability and Global Environmental Governance* (London: Routledge, 2003); Kristine Kern and Harriet Bulkeley, "Cities, Europeanization and Multi-level Governance: Governing Climate Change through Transnational Municipal Networks," *Journal of Common Market Studies* 47, no.2 (2009): 309–32.

16 Climate Alliance, *Our Members*, available online at http://www.klimabuend-nis.org/our_members0.0.html [accessed January 21, 2015].

17 Kern and Bulkeley, "Cities, Europeanization and Multi-level Governance."

18 Bulkeley and Betsill, *Cities and Climate Change*.

19 ICLEI, *Cities for Climate Protection (CCP) Campaign*, available online at http://archive.iclei.org/index.php?id=10829 [accessed January 21, 2015].

20 Energy Cities, *Energy Cities in Europe*, available online at http://www.energy-cities.eu/-Members- [accessed January 21, 2015].

21 Kern and Bulkeley, "Cities, Europeanization and Multi-level Governance."

22 The US Conference of Mayors Climate Protection Centre, *Mayors Leading the Way on Climate Protection*, available online at http://www.usmayors.org/climateprotection/revised/ [accessed January 21, 2015].

23 ICLEI Archive, *Kyoto City presents the World Mayors Council on Climate Change at the United Nations* (May 8, 2006), available online at http://www.archive.iclei.org/index.php?id=1487&tx_ttnews%5BpS%5D=1362742820&tx_ttnews%5Bpointer%5D=149&tx_ttnews%5Btt_news%5D=206&tx_ttnews%5BbackPid%5D=1556&cHash=8c79654456 [accessed January 21, 2015].

24 Covenant of Mayors, *Covenant of Mayors: committed to sustainable energy*, available online at http://www.covenantofmayors.eu/index_en.html [accessed January 21, 2015].

25 C40 Cities, *Our Partners and Funders*, available online at http://www.c40.org/partners [accessed January 21, 2015].

26 Clinton Foundation, *Energy Efficiency Program*, available online at http://www.clintonfoundation.org/our-work/clinton-climate-initiative/programs/built-environment [accessed January 21, 2015].

27 ICLEI, *Green Climate Cities Program: A Pathway to Urban Low-carbon Development*, available online at http://www.iclei.org/our-activities/our-agendas/low-carbon-city/gcc.html [accessed January 21, 2015].

28 World Bank, *Cities and Climate Change: An Urgent Agenda* (Washington, DC: World Bank, 2010).

29 UN-Habitat, *Global Report on Human Settlements: Cities and Climate Change* (Nairobi, Kenya: UN-Habitat, 2011).

30 Kern and Bulkeley, "Cities, Europeanization and Multi-level Governance," 319–20.

31 Energy Cities, *Study Tours*, available online at http://www.energy-cities.eu/-Study-Tours,14- [accessed January 21, 2015].

32 Harriet Bulkeley, "Urban Sustainability: Learning from Best Practice?," *Environment and Planning A* 38, no. 5 (2006): 235–54.

33 Bulkeley and Betsill, *Cities and Climate Change*.

34 Michele Betsill and Harriet Bulkeley, "Transnational Networks and Global Environmental Governance: The Cities for Climate Protection Program," *International Studies Quarterly* 48, no. 2 (2004): 471–93; Bulkeley, "Urban Sustainability: Learning from Best Practice?"

35 Climate Alliance, *Activity Report* (Frankfurt/Main: Climate Alliance, 2007).

36 Harriet Bulkeley, "Down to Earth: Local Government and Greenhouse Policy in Australia," *Australian Geographer* 31, no. 3 (2000): 289–308.

37 Kern and Bulkeley, "Cities, Europeanization and Multi-level Governance."

38 Bulkeley and Betsill, *Cities and Climate Change*.

39 Andonova and Levy, "Franchising Global Governance: Making Sense of the Johannesburg Type II Partnerships"; Bäckstrand, "Accountability of Networked Climate Governance"; Thorsten Benner, Wolfgang H. Reinicke, and Jan Martin Witte, "Multisectoral Networks in Global Governance";

Frank Biermann, Arthur P.J. Mol and Pieter Glasbergen, "Conclusion: Partnerships for Sustainability – Reflections on a Future Research Agenda," in *Partnerships, Governance and Sustainable Development, Reflections on Theory and Practice*, eds Frank Biermann, Arthur P.J. Mol, and Pieter Glasbergen (Cheltenham, UK: Edward Elgar, 2007), 288–300; Pattberg and Stripple, "Beyond the Public and Private Divide."

40 Bäckstrand, "Accountability of Networked Climate Governance," 77; Pattberg and Stripple, "Beyond the Public and Private Divide."

41 Bäckstrand, "Accountability of Networked Climate Governance," 89.

42 REEEP, *REEEP: A Brief Overview*, available online at http://www.reeep.org/reeep-brief-overview [accessed January 21, 2015].

43 REEEP, *Mission*, available online at http://www.reeep.org/mission [accessed January 21, 2015].

44 Bäckstrand, "Accountability of Networked Climate Governance," 90–1.

45 UNEP DTU Partnership, *Welcome to the UNEP DTU CDM/JI Pipeline Analysis and Database*, available online at http://cdmpipeline.org/ [accessed January 21, 2015].

46 Charlotte Streck, "New Partnerships in Global Environmental Policy: The Clean Development Mechanism," *Journal of Environment and Development* 13, no. 3 (2004): 295.

47 Streck, "New Partnerships in Global Environmental Policy," 297.

48 Ben Pearson, "Market Failure: Why the Clean Development Mechanism Won't Promote Clean Development," *Journal of Cleaner Production* 15, no. 2 (2007): 247–52.

49 Kenneth W. Abbott, "The Transnational Regime Complex for Climate Change," *Environment and Planning C: Government and Policy* 30, no. 4 (2012): 571–90.

50 The Climate Group, *States and Regions*, available online at http://www.theclimategroup.org/what-we-do/programs/States-and-Regions/ [accessed January 21, 2015].

51 The Climate Group, *Ten Years of The Climate Group*, available online at http://www.theclimategroup.org/our-achievements/ [accessed January 21, 2015].

52 John G. Ruggie, "Reconstituting the Global Public Domain: Issues, Actors and Practices," *European Journal of International Relations* 10, no. 4 (2004): 504.

53 Ruggie, "Reconstituting the Global Public Domain," 504.

54 Cashore *et al.*, *Governing through Markets*; Clapp, "The Privatisation of Global Environmental Governance: ISO 14001 and the Developing World"; Klaus Dingwerth, "North–South Parity in Global Governance: The Affirmative Procedures of the Forest Stewardship Council," *Global Governance: A Review of Multilateralism and International Organizations* 14, no. 1 (2008): 53–73; Pattberg and Stripple, "Beyond the Public and Private Divide."

55 Dingwerth, "North–South Parity in Global Governance," 608.

56 World Resources Institute, *Mind the Science, Mind the Gap: Aligning Corporate GHG Emissions Reduction Targets with Climate Science*, available online at http://www.wri.org/our-work/project/mind-science-mind-gap-aligning-corporate-ghg-emissions-reduction-targets-climate [accessed January 21, 2015].

57 Ingrid J. Visseren-Hamakers and Bas Arts, "Interaction Management by Partnerships: The Case of Biodiversity and Climate Change Governance System Interaction," *Paper prepared for the Private Environmental Regimes Conference*, 2008.

58 CCBA, *Projects*, available online at http://www.climate-standards.org/ category/projects/ [accessed January 21, 2015].

59 Bulkeley *et al.*, *Transnational Climate Change Governance*, 70.

60 Clapp, "The Privatization of Global Environmental Governance"; Peter Newell, "The Marketisation of Global Environmental Governance: Manifestations and Implications," in *The Crisis of Global Environmental Governance: Towards a New Political Economy of Sustainability*, eds Jacob Parks, Ken Conca, and Matthias Finger (London: Routledge, 2008), 77–96.

61 Ruggie, "Reconstituting the Global Public Domain," 504.

62 ICLEI Oceania, *Local Government Action on Climate Change: CCP Australia Measures Evaluation Report 2008* (Melbourne, Australia: ICLEI Oceana and Australian Government, 2008), available online at http://archive.iclei.org/ index.php?id=ccp-measures08 [accessed January 21, 2015].

63 Hoffmann, *Climate Governance at the Crossroads*.

64 Abbott, "The Transnational Regime Complex for Climate Change"; Bulkeley *et al.*, *Transnational Climate Change Governance*.

65 "IPCC Chapter 13, International Cooperation: Agreements and Instruments", in *Working Group III contribution to the IPCC Fifth Assessment Report "Climate Change 2014: Mitigation of Climate Change"*, accepted but not approved in detail by the 12th Session of Working Group III and the 39th Session of the IPCC on April 12, 2014 in Berlin, Germany (2014), 1012, available online at http://report.mitigation2014.org/drafts/final-draft-postplenary/ipcc_wg3_ar5_ final-draft_postplenary_chapter13.pdf [accessed January 21, 2015].

66 Peter Newell, "Civil Society, Corporate Accountability and the Politics of Climate Change," *Global Environmental Politics* 8, no. 3 (2008): 124–55.

4

COMMUNITY AND THE GOVERNING OF CLIMATE CHANGE

One long-standing feature of environmental governance in general is the involvement of community-based and "civil society" organizations in all aspects of politics as advocates, educators, implementers, and active citizens; as makers as well as shapers of policy.[1] It is unsurprising, then, that a wide array of social or community actors, including various voluntary groups, NGOs, and civil society institutions, have also been critical of the politics of climate change.[2] Because addressing climate change implies actions at all levels, and as we show in the Introduction, change in everyday patterns of production and consumption, engaging communities in mitigation and adaptation efforts, is also a key policy goal. At the most basic level, without the participation of the public—for example, in terms of their acquiescence to new forms of carbon regulation, their participation in carbon markets, or changing behavioral practices at home and at work—climate policy will fail to achieve the targeted reductions in GHG emissions. Urging communities to "do their bit," national and local governments, as well as a range of non-state actors, have sought to engage communities in responding to climate change. Social responses to climate change—much like those of the market (Chapter 5)—therefore involve a complex mixture of public and private authority, top-down direction, and bottom-up experimentation.

In this chapter, we focus on this spectrum of community-based responses and their role in the governance of climate change. First, we consider the ways in which governments have sought to engage the public in climate change. Here, we document a shift from a concern to educate individuals in order to change behavior towards various attempts to draw community expertise into the design and development of climate change responses. Second, we examine the ways in which place-based communities are being mobilized in response to climate change by (government) authorities. All too often, it seems, such schemes fail to engage with communities and tensions emerge between the realization of global objectives—for example, the reduction of GHG emissions—and locally based concerns and needs. Third, we turn to the example of Transition Towns (TT) to assess the emergence of grassroots responses to climate change. While concerns for social and environmental justice lie closer to the heart of such initiatives, we find that tensions still remain in seeking to govern the global and the local simultaneously.

Engaging communities: from ignorance to expertise

Since it first emerged on the policy agenda in the early 1990s, governments (and some non-governmental actors) have sought to mobilize community participation in the climate change issue. Despite some apparent consensus on the importance of engaging the public,[3] there are different views about what this should entail. Traditionally, it was thought that behavioral change would occur if communities were provided with information about the nature of environmental risks and what they could do to address them. More recently, approaches informed by assumptions about "information deficits" and "ignorant publics" have been critiqued and the importance of basing policy on community knowledge and concerns has been recognized.[4] In parallel, research suggests that seeking to engage individuals in action on climate change requires an engagement with the ways in which GHG emissions are produced through the practices that comprise everyday life.[5] In this section, we trace these shifts and their implications for governing climate change.

As public concern for environmental issues grew during the 1970s and 1980s, an apparent paradox emerged. On the one hand, opinion polls and surveys seemed to indicate that environmental matters—and increasingly those of a global nature, such as climate change—were attracting high levels of concern amongst the public. On the other hand, the public appeared to be relatively ignorant about the scientific basis and implications of these issues, and at the same time unwilling to engage in behavioral change to address them.[6] In this context, the conviction emerged in policy circles that there was a "deficit" of public knowledge about the issue, spurring the development of environmental education campaigns in Europe, North America, and Australia. One example is the "Helping the Earth Begins at Home" campaign, run in the United Kingdom during the 1990s. In this campaign, newspaper and television adverts provided information about the causes of global warming (as it was then commonly referred to), and about the potential for behavioral changes at home to save energy, save money, and reduce emissions of GHG.[7]

BOX 4.1 THE GOVERNANCE TRAP IN CLIMATE POLICY

In seeking to avoid the political risks of taking long-term action, governments have frequently responded to the need to act on climate change by placing responsibility back onto individuals, communities, and firms in the context of proposals for carbon foot-printing, carbon disclosure for firms, and personal carbon allowances.[a] For individuals, research suggests that the majority of people in the United Kingdom believe that climate change is too big a problem for individuals to tackle and that responsibility lies with national governments. The result is a "governance trap" in which both the governing and the governed seek action from the other, but none is forthcoming.[b]

Sources:
[a] See, for example, proposals for Tradable Energy Quotas, e.g. David Fleming and Shaun Chamberlain, Tradable Energy Quotas (London: All Party Parliamentary Group on Peak Oil and The Lean Economy Connection, 2011).
[b] Alexa Spence, Dan Venables, Nick Pidgeon, Wouter Poortinga, and Christina Demski, *Public Perceptions of Climate Change and Energy Futures in Britain: Summary Findings of a Survey Conducted in January–March 2010*, Technical Report (Cardiff University: Understanding Risk Working Paper 10–01).

Yet, despite the high levels of exposure in the media, Steve Hinchliffe found that the campaign was largely ineffective.[8] In focusing on the provision of information, the campaign, like many other initiatives, had neglected the numerous other factors which shape behavioral change, including issues of responsibility, trust, and efficacy. For example, in their exploration of public understanding of global environmental issues in the Surselva region of Switzerland, Carlo Jaeger *et al.* conclude that knowledge about climate change is a less important factor in determining behavior than social networks and rules that sanction and enable mitigating actions.[9] Analysis by Willet Kempton *et al.* found that public understandings of climate change in the United States were based on fundamental moral and religious views on the relation between nature and humanity, the rights of other species, humanity's right to change or manage nature, and our society's responsibility for future generations.[10] More recent studies have sustained this view that public engagement in environmental issues, and climate change in particular, is shaped by a range of individual and social factors and that the provision of information alone is unlikely to have much effect on behavior (see Box 4.1).

Recognition of the flaws of the "information deficit" approach has led to calls for new approaches to engage the public with the issue of climate change. First, advocates argued for an approach to involving communities that recognized and valued their experiences and knowledge, and which facilitated debate about policy choices.[11] One reason underpinning this shift was the recognition that the public may have forms of knowledge which would prove valuable in understanding and responding to environmental risks. For example, Judith Petts and Catherine Brooks suggest that lay people may be "local technical experts,"[12] using the case of how cyclists have questioned the validity of local air quality modeling and used their experience of city streets at the micro-scale to provide an alternative map of urban pollution.[13] Another reason was the recognition that the public's view of the practical, ethical, and political aspects of environmental problems might be as significant as understanding the scientific issues at hand. Importantly, it was thought that this approach "might help not only to identify or implement solutions but to define, or reframe, what the problems actually are."[14]

One area of climate change governance where this more participatory approach is beginning to be adopted is in relation to climate change adaptation.[15] In the Philippines, community-based disaster preparedness (CBDP) approaches have been used by the Red Cross as a means of reducing vulnerability and enhancing resilience to the impacts of climate change.[16] The CBDP approaches seek to "build on existing local knowledge and experience, as well as the resources, coping and adaptive strategies of local people."[17] In the case of the Philippines, CBDP involved projects such as constructing flood defenses and training in disaster management skills in order to provide skills and experience for longer term "flexible and incremental" approaches to climate adaptation.[18] A similar approach, Vulnerability and Capacity Assessment (VCA), has been used by the Red Cross in Vietnam and Indonesia.[19] It is carried out at the level of villages and urban neighborhoods, and uses participatory rapid appraisal (PRA) tools to diagnose vulnerabilities, assess a community's risk priorities, and work together with the people to devise ways of increasing their capacities to resist hazard impacts.[20] Articulating one of the central arguments voiced in support of such participatory and deliberative techniques, Maarten K. van Aalst, Terry Cannon, and Ian Burton argue that a key purpose of the approach is to:

catalyze a process that empowers the people in the community and supports their capacity to alter their own situation. Through engagement with the grass roots, the activities that emerge will have the people's 'ownership' and participation, be based on trust and therefore have more chance of success.[21]

Their investigation of the use of such approaches found, however, a tension between the aims of local community empowerment and the need to engage with the science of climate change impacts, which required expert-led processes of knowledge dissemination.[22] Further tensions emerged in the process of community engagement in the Philippines, where the idea of communities as homogeneous within the CBDP discourse tended to subsume competing interests and priorities within and between community groups while also neglecting structural processes over which local communities have little if any control. At the same time, the rhetoric of building adaptive capacity implicitly assumes that such processes will create more "productive, participatory relations with government agencies."[23] In this manner, far from being autonomous from the central state, community-based initiatives provide a key means through which the state seeks to govern climate change, a point to which we return below.

A second shift in thinking about the nature of public engagement with climate change, that has been prompted by dissatisfaction with the information deficit approach, has focused on the importance of understanding the ways in which the forms of individual behavior, that appear to lead to GHG emissions, are intimately tied up with everyday practices. Rather than conceiving of individuals as forming attitudes that lead to particular forms of behavior through which people make (more or less) rational choices about their actions in relation to climate change, Elizabeth Shove argues that we need to move beyond this "ABC" model and consider how the production of GHG emissions is constituted through practices such as cooking, washing clothes, entertaining and driving.[24] From this perspective, changing actions at the individual or household level that produce GHG emissions entails understanding how and why such practices persist and come to be routine.

While the way in which it has been undertaken has shifted over time, this overview suggests that engaging communities on the issue of climate change has been seen as central to the implementation of policy at national and local levels, either because of a need to educate the public in order to achieve behavioral change (for example, reducing car travel and energy use), because of the ways in which public knowledge might be able to inform policy design, or more recently from an interest in shifting the systems of provision and consumption through which GHG emissions are produced. We can see that involving the public is, therefore, a key means through which such actors seek to govern climate change.

Governing place, governing community

Public education and engagement do not exhaust the means by which policy makers have sought to govern climate change. The importance of "community" as a site of governance has been highlighted by governmentality scholars, who point to the ways in which the idea is used to mobilize particular practices and aspirations that authorities of various sorts consider desirable.[25] In particular, the rhetoric of community invokes a sense of "self-help" and "self-reliance"[26] in which communities are encouraged to take responsibility for addressing policy issues such as climate change. In this section, we examine two examples of such community-based responses to governing climate change—small-scale forestry projects[27] and renewable energy schemes[28] —and consider the implications for how we might understand by whom and with what implications climate change is governed.

Community forestry and carbon governance

Under the terms of UNFCCC and the Kyoto Protocol, projects which involve reforestation or afforestation—the conversion of land to forests or the rehabilitation of forests—and the consequent removal of carbon dioxide from the atmosphere—carbon sequestration—were included as a means of reaching national targets for emission reductions under Activities Implemented Jointly (AIJ) and the subsequent CDM (see Chapters 1 and 2). The imperative to effectively manage and renew forest resources has long been a mainstay of conservation and development discourses.[29] Since the 1970s, the argument has evolved that communities need to be involved in the management of forests both because of their expertise and because without such involvement efforts will be ineffective at best or deliberately undermined at worst. Attempts at "fortress conservation"—where communities are kept on the outside of conserved areas—have been shown to fail, as communities dependent upon forest resources continue to seek their livelihoods through these means.[30] The language and approach of the climate change regime also recognizes the importance of including communities in the processes of carbon sequestration and of delivering "side-benefits" in terms of development.[31]

Despite these mechanisms, only a few small-scale forestry projects were developed under the mechanisms of the UNFCCC and the Kyoto Protocol. Some 30 forest sinks projects were tested under the UNFCCC AIJ pilot phase of which several explicitly targeted small-holders and low income producers aiming to provide dual benefits of global climate protection and local development benefits.[32] Under the CDM, a total of 68 forestry projects have so far been registered, although they are more prevalent in the voluntary carbon offset market.[33] The development of the Reducing Emissions from Deforestation and Forest Degradation (REDD+)[34] mechanism of the UNFCCC has also served to place forestry interventions as central to the governing of climate change, with the emergence of a plethora of multilateral and bilateral funding arrangements, partnerships, and projects being directed towards developing countries and in turn the potential for community-based projects. These are meant to deliver both decarbonization and additional social and environmental benefits. However, analysis suggests that the top-down nature of these initiatives, being driven primarily by international agencies and national governments, has meant that "pilot forest carbon projects have tended to fall short of their development objectives by failing to include local stakeholders in decision making and to ensure their buy-in early on in the project design."[35]

The case of community forestry management in Mexico illustrates some of the complexities involved in seeking to govern climate change through the enrolment of local communities and places. In the mid-1980s, and in the context of a high rate of deforestation, the Mexican government began to promote community forestry and, more recently, have developed schemes in which local communities receive financial reward for the "ecosystem services" that the conservation and renewal of forest areas delivers.[36] In 2003, one such scheme, Payments for Hydrological Services, was established by a government ministry and the National Institute of Ecology. Subsequently, and following the lobbying of central government by various peasant- and forest-based organizations, in 2004, a program of Payments for Carbon, Biodiversity and Agro-forestry services (PSA-CABSA) was established, reflecting at least some degree of support from local communities for recognizing their forest management activities in these terms. Evidence suggests that such projects have delivered considerable economic benefits to local communities and some notable social benefits, as well as carbon sequestration (see Box 4.2 for one example).[37] The involvement and support of communities also seems to have been relatively high, a finding explained in part by the institutional design of the scheme which involved community-based organizations in establishing the rules of the game, independent evaluations of compliance, implementation rules that have been enforced and have minimized illegal logging, and rights of appeal for the providers of ecosystem services. While there are questions about the ways in which ecosystem services have been accounted for and about the long-term financial viability of the PSA-CABSA, the preliminary assessment of the scheme was positive.

BOX 4.2 COMMUNITY FORESTRY AND DEVELOPMENT

San Bartolomé Loxicha, an indigenous Zapotec community located in the state of Oaxaca, Mexico encompasses over 14,000 hectares and has over 2,250 inhabitants. The main economic activities are coffee cultivation and commercial logging. In 2004, a carbon project involving the plantation of 66,000 pines in 272 hectares of the forest commons was approved for implementation. The project was considered an opportunity for complementing ongoing reforestation and conservation activities. The total investment from the program for Payments for Carbon, Biodiversity and Agro-forestry services has amounted to over MX$2.7 million (or US$0.2 million), of which over 70 percent has reached the community. The community assembly was involved in determining how the project funding should be distributed, and 20 percent was given to the Milenio Coffee Producers Organization, most of whose 100 farmers were involved in carbon project activities, with the remaining 80 percent distributed among the farmers who participated in tree planting.

Source: Esteve Corbera, Carmen González Soberanis, and Katrina Brown, "Institutional Dimensions of Payments for Ecosystem Services: an Analysis of Mexico's Carbon Forestry Programme," *Ecological Economics* 68, no. 3 (2009): 743–61.

However, changes to the scheme in the light of international and national demands to better account for carbon services and to secure external flows of financing may serve to undermine the benefits of community involvement which have been secured. In 2006, the guidance for carbon service projects changed quite substantially, following the criteria established by the CDM concerning the size of projects involved, and the timing and extent of deforestation while funding was limited to project design with external investors required to purchase the carbon saved in these projects.[38] These changes reflected both the international guidance on forest projects from the CDM and "the interest of the Mexican government to support projects which may potentially become sources of voluntary and CDM carbon offsets."[39] Analysis suggests that this move has gone "against the interests of Mexican civil organizations," since under the new rules there "has been a reduction in the number of project applications, and an increase in the rate of applications' rejections," with the result of undermining "communities' ability to access carbon payments."[40] This example shows how decisions concerning climate governance taken at an international level can have significant implications for local communities and places, raising questions about whose resources are being governed, and whose interests are being served, by such governance mechanisms.

As we saw in Chapter 2, others have raised similar deep-seated concerns about the emerging carbon market and the ways in which communities, particularly in the global South, may be affected.[41] Adam Bumpus and Diana Liverman argue that the process of the commodification of carbon—its extraction from local contexts and circulation in global markets—is following a neo-liberal logic concerned with creating profit at the expense of both its effectiveness in terms of reducing GHG emissions and its implications for local communities.[42] Because of the economic logic of the CDM, and indeed of wider systems of ecosystem service payments, the implementation of CDM projects has followed the "avenues of the most profitable geographical locations," while the sustainable development benefits which are supposed to also accrue are neglected.[43] Once the value of a resource is changed and it becomes of commercial value to international investors, communities home to those resources find themselves under pressure. The introduction of REDD+ has brought a much stronger focus on realizing the benefits of forestry projects for communities. The Mpingo Conservation and Development Initiative in Tanzania, for instance, has sought to leverage REDD+ as a means of expanding their successful Forest Stewardship Scheme project which is based on the sustainable and equitable harvest of timber.[44] Their experience suggests that REDD+ is both enabling NGOs to work with communities to identify the causes of deforestation—in this case the assumed cause of charcoal production was found to be less important than the deliberate use of fire as a farming technique—and enabling access to additional resources for realizing the economic value of forests for communities. Yet, the project was demanding in terms of assessing the carbon savings potential, selecting the appropriate validation scheme from the multiple choices available, and in gaining community trust. An initial assessment of the benefits being derived by communities from REDD+ finds that:

many early REDD+ projects are delivering measurable socio-economic benefits by enhancing populations' tenure security and facilitating their empowerment through meaningful participation in REDD+ project design and implementation . . . [but] to date, projects have produced only modest opportunity benefits (jobs, income) for local populations.[45]

This suggests that while such projects can bring benefits, their design and implementation are critical in terms of determining how and for whom such benefits are realized.

Seeking to involve communities in the governing of climate change through small-scale forestry projects has been a strategy deployed by governments and the international community, and, in part, one welcomed by some of the communities involved. However, it is a process that raises complex questions about the basis upon which communities should be involved, and about the tensions between local community needs and the imperatives of international policy and carbon markets. While on the surface, a synergy between community-based forestry projects, sustainable development, and carbon sequestration appears to be a matter of common sense, the processes and practices involved reveal conflicting agendas, priorities and outcomes, and raise important questions over the nature and distribution of the benefits of such schemes.

Community power: renewable energy in the United Kingdom

In the United Kingdom, since the privatization of the energy generation and supply system in the 1980s, the development and deployment of renewable energy technologies has traditionally been assumed to be the preserve of the private sector, albeit subject to government mandate concerning the proportion of renewable energy in the supply mix. However, since the development of the 2003 Energy White Paper, the importance of community involvement in the provision of renewable energy has increasingly been stressed. Moving beyond exhortations to consult or engage communities in decisions over the siting of renewable energy generation technologies (though this remains an important rhetoric), this new theme incorporates "notions of community led, controlled and owned renewable energy installation development"[46] and has been manifest in a series of government-funded programs, including the Community Action for Energy program, Community Renewables Initiative, Clear Skies, and Community Energy scheme.[47] Gordon Walker and colleagues found that in 2004 there were over 500 ongoing or completed projects supported by these programs or initiatives and others with the word "community" in their title and/or rationale in the United Kingdom.[48] These included projects in which there was a degree of community ownership, through cooperatives, charities, trusts, or other arrangements, or where co-ownership between a private company and community takes place. One of the best known examples of the former in the United Kingdom is the Baywind cooperative,[49] in which people within and beyond the local community become members of the cooperative and buy shares to finance the project.[50] In addition to community ownership, community involvement in renewable energy projects was manifest in two other ways: first, in terms of the involvement of communities in the development and running of projects, and second, in terms of the distribution of the benefits of such schemes, for example "providing jobs, contributing to local regeneration or providing an educational resource."[51]

Despite significant variation in how the term was used, the salience of the theme of "community" in the provision of renewable energy in the United Kingdom appears to have been high, with a number of significant funding streams dedicated to their realization and several hundred projects established or underway. In seeking to account for this phenomenon, Gordon Walker *et al.* identify four explanations.[52] First, developing a community-basis to renewable energy generation was regarded as a means of overcoming public opposition to renewable energy, particularly in the wake of the conflicts over the siting of onshore wind farms that has occurred in the United Kingdom.[53] Second, a community-based approach allowed the government to stimulate the market for renewable energy, regarded as critical in the context of carbon reduction targets and the need to improve skills and capacities with regard to newer, micro-generation, technologies. A third rationale lay with the predominantly rural nature of the projects implemented, based on a perceived need to stimulate economic growth and security in declining rural areas. Finally, there was a sense that communities should be involved, in a normative sense, because it was a legitimate and democratic means through which decisions about energy futures should be made.[54] These explanations point once again to the significance of community as a site which is crucial for the achievement of government policy objectives for climate change, including the United Kingdom's targets for meeting 20 percent of electricity generation from renewable sources by 2020.

In 2010, further measures were introduced to meet this aim, including the introduction of a feed-in-tariff (FIT) that provides a payment for the generation and export of electricity from small-scale renewable energy installations. The introduction of the FIT stimulated a significant rise in the number of renewable energy installations at the household and community scale, in particular solar photovoltaics (PV). In 2011, the subsidy which had been at a rate of 43.3p was lowered to 21p per kilowatt hour, doubling the period over which an installation would "payback" its costs.[55] The FIT applicable to new installations has been progressively reduced in line with the number and capacity of installations that have been made, so that between April and July 2014, the rate for PV stood at 14.38p/kWh, or 6.38p/kWh if the building where it was installed did not meet a minimum energy performance rating.[56] The subsidy rates for other small-scale renewables have also been reduced, but rates for micro-hydro, wind, and micro combined heat and power (mCHP) were all above solar PV, reflecting their more limited deployment in the United Kingdom. While the FIT was not focused on community renewables per se, its introduction provided another means of support for community organizations interested in engaging with climate change and/or with addressing local concerns for securing affordable energy supply. In Oxford, the Low Carbon West Oxford group established the West Oxford Community Renewables (WOCoRe), "an Industrial and Provident society for the benefit of the community, [which] raises money from a mix of government grants, prize money and its own share offer."[57] Low Carbon West Oxford secured over £900,000 in 2009 through the Department for Energy and Climate Change's Low Carbon Communities program and the Big Green Challenge competition run by the UK-based charity NESTA. Photovoltaic systems have been installed on schools and community buildings, and a project to develop a micro-hydro power station on the River Thames at Osney is underway. At the same time, the work of Low Carbon West Oxford focuses on establishing different norms around low carbon living, such as eating seasonally, reducing waste, improving housing conditions, and building stronger community ties. These examples illustrate how community projects become essential to, and enrolled in, these wider policy agendas, but also retain the possibility of governing climate change differently, because of the democratic mandate they engender.

Through these case studies of carbon forestry and renewable energy, we can see that the reasons for "community-based" climate governance stem not only from efforts to displace responsibilities onto the community, but also as part of a much more explicit strategy to implement policy and meet climate governance objectives devised at other scales. However, other forms of community-based climate governance—primarily emerging from outside of the state—have provided the space for alternative approaches to addressing climate change, and it is to these that we now turn.

Communities governing climate change

In addition to initiatives to engage communities that have emerged from within the state, communities have also acted as a site for independent responses to climate change. These community-based climate governance initiatives range in size and scale from individual groups of households or neighborhoods to transnational networks seeking to connect communities across national boundaries (see Chapter 3). Some are organized and orchestrated by third sector and non-governmental organizations, while others originate in the concerns and spontaneous actions of individuals. Despite their relatively low profile and limited reach, these community-based initiatives provide a means through which individuals are becoming directly involved in addressing climate change—a level of engagement that has so far eluded mainstream national and international responses to the issue. At the same time, such initiatives provide a source of alternative means of framing and acting on climate change, which offer a basis for contesting orthodox policy approaches and which may provide a source of social and technical innovation at other scales of governance. Here we consider one such example—Transition Towns—in order to examine the implications for climate governance.

Transition Towns

> A Transition Initiative is a community . . . working together to look Peak Oil and Climate Change squarely in the eye and address this BIG question: for all those aspects of life that this community needs in order to sustain itself and thrive, how do we significantly increase resilience (to mitigate the effects of Peak Oil) and drastically reduce carbon emissions (to mitigate the effects of Climate Change)?[58]

The idea of a "transition" from oil-based to low-carbon societies as a localized movement originated in Kinsale, Ireland, in 2005, and was adopted by the town of Totnes, in Devon, England, in 2006 through the work of Rob Hopkins, a permaculture teacher. The central idea, as illustrated in the quote above taken from the TT website, is that communities need to face the realities of "peak oil"—preparing for a future world without oil resources—as well as significantly reducing GHG emissions. The TT movement links these two issues together, arguing for the positive benefits that can accrue from localizing economies through, for example, the production of local sources of food and energy. Following Totnes, several other communities in Southwest England took up the initiative and in 2007 a Transition Network was established in order to support the spread of the ideas. By 2008, some 100 communities had joined the network, primarily based in the United Kingdom, but also including the United States, Australia, Japan, and Chile, and by 2014 this number had reached over 470, with groups also starting in Asia, India, and South Africa.[59] In this process, the Transition Network has become a more formal entity,[60] and a process of signing up to 16 criteria has now been adopted for those communities wishing to become part of the movement (see Box 4.3). These criteria set out "demands for mainly local commitments" that "resonate with the duties inherent in communitarian theories of citizenship,"[61] in which obligations are due first and foremost to the community within which individuals reside.

A wide range of actions and activities are undertaken under the banner of TT, including a focus on local food production, health, transport, and energy. For example, in Totnes, a Garden Share project has been established that "matches keen, enthusiastic and committed gardeners and local garden owners who want to see their gardens being used more productively. The gardener and garden owner enter into an agreement about times, arrangements, security and the sharing of garden produce."[62] In Brixton, London, a Food and Growing group has been set up, also with a focus on food issues, where members are involved in "finding out about local food suppliers and more about how to start growing their own food; reskilling (cooking, growing, permaculture, food preservation); [and] starting their own community growing and composting projects."[63] Also in Brixton, the initial formation of a Buildings and Energy group led to the development of Brixton Energy, a not-for-profit energy company which created a community investment vehicle through which to secure funding to generate energy within the community through the installation of PV, while in Berera, Kentucky, United States, the group has established a Resilient Household project, aimed to assist residents to adapt to current and future environmental risks.[64]

BOX 4.3 TRANSITION NETWORK MEMBERSHIP

The criteria and process for membership of the Transition Network, as available on their website, is as follows:

1 An understanding of peak oil and climate change as twin drivers (to be written into constitution or governing documents).
2 A group of 4–5 people willing to step into leadership roles (not just the boundless enthusiasm of a single person).

3   We recommend—time and resources permitting—that at least two
members of the core team aim to attend the two day Training for
Transition course. These are now available internationally, listed
either here or on the National Transition Hub for your country.

4   A potentially strong connection to the local council.

5   An initial understanding of the 12 ingredients to becoming a TT.

6   A commitment to ask for help when needed.

7   A commitment to regularly update your Transition Initiative
web presence—either the "community microsite" (collaborative
workspace on the web that we'll make available to you), or your
own website.

8   A commitment to make periodic contributions to a blog (the
world will be watching) either on the Transition Network site
itself or on one that we can aggregate onto the site.

9   A commitment, once you're into the Transition, for your group
to give at least two presentations to other communities in your
vicinity that are considering embarking on this journey—a sort
of "here's what we did" or "here's how it was for us" talk

10 A commitment to network with other TTs.

11 A commitment to work cooperatively with neighbouring TTs.

12 Minimal conflicts of interests in the core team.

13 A commitment to work with the Transition Network or your
National Transition Hub regarding grant applications for funding from national grant giving bodies. Your own local trusts are,
of course, yours to deal with as you see fit.

14 A commitment to strive for inclusivity across your entire initiative. We're aware that we need to strengthen this point in
response to concerns about extreme political groups becoming involved in transition initiatives. One way of doing this is
for your core group to explicitly state their support for the UN
Declaration of Human Rights (General Assembly resolution 217
A (III) of December 10, 1948). You could add this to your constitution (when finalized) so that extreme political groups that have
discrimination as a key value cannot participate in the decision
making bodies within your transition initiative.

15 A recognition that although your entire county or district may
need to go through transition, the first place for you to start is
in your local community. It may be that eventually the number
of transitioning communities in your area warrant some central

group to help provide local support, but this will emerge over time, rather than be imposed. (This point was inserted in response to the several instances of people rushing off to transition their entire county/region rather than their local community.) Further criteria apply to initiating/coordinating hubs—these can be discussed in person.

16 And finally, we recommend that at least one person on the core team should have attended a permaculture design course . . . it really does seem to make a difference.

Source: Criteria and process for becoming an "official" Transition Initiative, available online at https://www.transitionnetwork.org/support/becoming-official [accessed February 10, 2015].

While the success of individual TT initiatives in terms of its impact on reducing emissions of GHG is both hard to measure and currently premature to evaluate, it is clear that the movement has generated significant interest. The growth of the network, from one or two cases in 2006 to nearly 500 in 2014, is one measure of its impact, but so too are the relatively large numbers of people attending information events in the transition towns (in many cases, several hundred people are involved in the launch or publicity events in any one town). However, whether this interest can be sustained as individual TT move from the dissemination of information to projects on the ground remains to be seen. At the same time, the movement has provided an alternative means of framing climate change as a "governance" problem—one that focuses on consumption rather than the production of GHG emissions, and on the local rather than global scale—that has provided the basis for contesting orthodox accounts of what the climate governance problem entails. Governance experiments such as this that bubble up "from below" show that governance, even around a problem as complex as climate change, is not only constructed above by policy elites where communities passively react to global political initiatives.[65] They also proactively create alternatives and produce immediate forms of action, often fuelled by a frustration with the slowness and inadequacy of existing responses.

Governance issues and challenges

In this chapter, we have suggested that alongside a growing interest in "market"-based solutions to the climate problem (Chapters 1 and 5), community is becoming an important site in the governing of climate change. A variety of ways in which state and non-state actors seek to engage communities, from education campaigns, to participatory processes, projects, and social movements, can now be found. We find that such initiatives have been driven by attempts to implement policy, by a rationale that seeks to mobilize "responsible" communities into governing climate change outside of the direct control of the state, and also by actors seeking to create an alternative politics of climate change. Community-based initiatives, unlike other forms of climate governance, have succeeded in generating a degree of public engagement with the issue of climate change. However, they are not without challenges in terms of effectiveness, legitimacy, and equity, and it is to these issues that we now turn.

The first issue in terms of the impact and effectiveness of community-based climate governance relates to the different levels of success in engaging the public which can be found across different approaches. Attempts to shift behavior through education campaigns have been found to be largely ineffective, while, on the other hand, community-based projects—such as those discussed here in terms of forestry and renewable energy—have had a much higher degree of success in terms of the number of participants and projects created, albeit remaining small in scale and few in number. This suggests that those schemes which seek to target individual members of the community may have less impact than those that focus on the community scale and seek to achieve change at this level of social organization. It may also be the case, as with the example of community forestry, that the potential material benefits that accrue to communities willing to participate in a project encourage them to do so. Likewise, communities expected to host "clean energy" projects such as wind farms are more likely to oppose them if they do not directly benefit and the electricity generated is transmitted elsewhere.

In terms of the impacts of the initiatives themselves, each has been successful in relation to some goals, for example in the spread of information about climate change and peak oil (TT), in terms of the promotion and development of demonstration projects (renewable energy in the United Kingdom), or in terms of generating income (small-scale forestry projects in Mexico). However, the impacts of these initiatives and others like them, in terms of reducing GHG emissions and achieving other sustainable development benefits, are less clear. First, such schemes remain—perhaps necessarily—small in scale and their effects highly uneven. Second, accounting for emissions savings and their additionality is challenging, given the range of factors that may be shaping individual behavior, shifts in everyday practice, investment decisions, and the emergence of new forms of energy technology. Third, there is evidence that some of the progressive goals of such initiatives (of community involvement, in the case of renewable energy in the United Kingdom, or of wider sustainable development objectives in the case of small-scale forestry) are being neglected in state-led community governance initiatives, suggesting that such schemes remain predominantly a means through which the state seeks to further its own interests in terms of climate governance, rather than providing arenas in which community goals can also be pursued. Community-led initiatives, such as the TT example used here, may be more able to retain the broader goals of social and environmental justice that frequently provide the basis for their development in the first place. However, this raises questions as to whether their impact will remain confined to the margins of formal politics, with little impact on mainstream approaches to climate governance or the vast bulk of GHG emissions. By their very nature they are voluntary and so communities—if they choose—can opt to do nothing in the absence of pressure to do otherwise.

In terms of accountability, community-based initiatives appear, at least on the surface, to offer a genuine means through which the public can be engaged on the issue of climate change. However, challenges arise in terms of how responsibility for addressing climate change is allocated in such schemes and the extent to which there is potential for genuine engagement in the framing and implementation of climate policy. Seeking to place responsibility on individuals and their behavior rather than wider systemic and structural processes may in fact be detrimental to engaging the public in climate governance, leading to a sense of disempowerment and exacerbating the "governance trap" described above (Box 4.1).[66] Rather than being a means through which publics are able to hold those in authority to account for climate change governance, community-based initiatives could be seen as a means through which state (and non-state) actors seek to shift responsibility, and with it accountability, to individuals, households, and particular places. This may serve to shift accountability from actors which preside over significant sources of GHG emissions and with the capacity to reduce vulnerability—such as nation-states and large corporations—to those who have little in the way of power to address either the causes or consequences of climate change—for example forest-based peoples in Mexico or rural communities in the United Kingdom. Moreover, even where community-based schemes enable external authorities to be held to account for their actions on climate change, the limited nature of participation in such schemes coupled with restrictions on what is "open" for negotiation can reduce the accountability of climate change governance. For example, in Mexico, changes in rules on carbon sequestration accounting, or on the funding available for renewable energy projects in the United Kingdom were beyond the remit of the communities involved, meaning that the answerability of central authorities to the communities involved in these schemes was limited. In this manner, the use of "community-based" projects by external authorities could function as a smokescreen for other agendas (for example, the promotion of wind energy in the United Kingdom despite "community" protests). Initiatives which have emerged at the grassroots level potentially have accountability built in, through processes of direct participation which allow people to engage or not, but here the key accountability challenge is one of enforceability—reliant on voluntary participation, they may fall short of achieving their ambitions.

These issues of accountability are intimately connected to those of equity in community-based initiatives. At issue here is how, on what grounds, and by whom, the terms of community engagement are established, and with what consequent implications for the distribution of costs and benefits. In particular, the case studies reviewed in this chapter suggest that there are profound equity implications that arise from the interplay of international and national policy agendas with local projects for addressing climate change. For example, in the case of Mexican CDM projects, shifts in the requirements for carbon accounting externally had significant implications for the social and environmental benefits of forest-carbon sequestration. At the same time, seeking to address climate change in certain places may have inequitable geographical impacts, as, for example, benefits from carbon forestry accrue to some communities and not others, some places experience the advantages (or disadvantages) of renewable energy generation, while the localization of food production, promoted by TT, has the potential to create negative implications for farmers in the global South. Community-based initiatives to address climate change are, therefore, not free from the politics of interest, and their development creates both winners and losers, as with all the aspects of climate governance that we consider in this book.

In this chapter, we have suggested that community is becoming a key site in the governing of climate change—a process that warrants attention in its own right, but that also has potentially significant implications for how we conceive of (global) climate governance. In regarding community as a site of climate governance, we have suggested that there is a need to reconsider the way in which the state operates. Rather than being confined to particular institutional boundaries, we have suggested that the state seeks to extend its reach through the transfer of responsibility for climate governance to sites of community. However, this extension of the state, and the multiple means through which climate change is being framed as a governance problem within community-based initiatives, raises questions about the limits of climate governance. While, as we outlined in the Introduction, a conception of global climate governance which confines itself to the global scale and to state-based institutions is no longer adequate, the question could also be raised as to whether everything—from a community garden project to an isolated wind turbine—should be considered as evidence of climate governance. In this context, determining why, and with what implications, particular initiatives are framed as a response to climate change, becomes ever more important. What is clear, however, is that alongside a growing "low carbon economy" (Chapter 5) we are witnessing the emergence of a "low carbon society" in which projects and initiatives of all shapes and sizes are increasingly justified in the name of climate change.

Notes

1 Ken Conca, "Greening the UN: Environmental Organizations and the UN System," *Third World Quarterly* 16, no. 3 (1995): 103–19; Thomas Princen and Matthias Finger, *Environmental NGOs in World Politics* (London: Routledge, 1994); Paul Wapner, *Environmental Activism and World Civic Politics* (Albany: State University of New York Press, 1996).

2 Matthew R. Auer, "Who Participates in Global Environmental Governance? Partial Answers From International Relations Theory," *Policy Sciences* 33, no. 2 (2000): 163.

3 Susan Owens, "Engaging the Public: Information and Deliberation in Environmental Policy," *Environment and Planning A* 32, no. 7 (2000): 1141–8.

4 Brian Wynne, "May the Sheep Graze Safely? A Reflexive View of the Expert–Lay Divide" in *Risk, Environment and Modernity: Towards a New Ecology*, eds Scott Lash, Bronislaw Szerszynski, and Brian Wynne (London: Sage, 1996), 44–83; Simon Joss, ed., "Public Participation in Science and Technology," special issue, *Science and Public Policy* 26, no. 5 (1999); Brian Wynne, "Creating Public Alienation: Expert Cultures of Risk and Ethics on GMOs," *Science as Culture* 10, no. 4 (2001): 445–81.

5 Elizabeth Shove, "Beyond the ABC: Climate Change Policy and Theories of Social Change," *Environment and Planning A* 42, no. 6 (2010): 1273–85.

6 Irene Lorenzoni, Sophie Nicholson-Cole, and Lorraine Whitmarsh, "Barriers Perceived to Engaging with Climate Change Among the UK Public and their Policy Implications," *Global Environmental Change: Human and Policy Dimensions* 17, no. 3/4 (2007): 445–59.

7 Steve Hinchliffe, "Helping the Earth Begins at Home: The Social Construction of Socio-Environmental Responsibilities," *Global Environmental Change— Human and Policy Dimensions* 6, no. 1 (1996): 53–62.

8 Hinchliffe, "Helping the Earth Begins at Home."

9 Carlo Jaeger, Gregor Durrenberger, Hans Kastenholz, and Bernhard Truffer, "Determinants of Environmental Action With Regard to Climatic-Change," *Climatic Change* 23, no. 3 (1993): 193–211.

10 Willet Kempton, James Boster, and Jennifer Hartley, *Environmental Values in American Culture* (Boston, Mass.: MIT Press, 1995).

11 Owens, "Engaging the Public"; Walter Baber and Robert V. Bartlett, *Deliberative Environmental Politics: Democracy and Ecological Rationality* (Cambridge, Mass.: MIT Press, 2005); Minu Hemmati, *Multi-Stakeholder Processes for Governance and Accountability* (London: Earthscan, 2002).

12 Judith Petts and Catherine Brooks, "Expert Conceptualizations of the Role of Lay Knowledge in Environmental Decision Making: Challenges for Deliberative Democracy," *Environment and Planning A* 38, no. 6 (2006): 1047–59.

13 Stephen Yearly, Steve Cinderby, John Forrester, Peter Bailey, and Paul Rosen, "Participatory Modelling and the Local Governance of the Politics of UK Air Pollution: a Three-City Case Study," *Environmental Values* 12, no. 2 (2003): 247–62.

14 Owens, "Engaging the Public," 1144.

15 Roger Few, Kate Brown, and Emma Tomkins, "Public Participation and Climate Change Adaptation: Avoiding the Illusion of Inclusion," *Climate Policy* 7, no. 1 (2007): 46–59.

16 John Allen, "The Whereabouts of Power: Politics, Government and Space," *Geografiska Annaler* 86B, no.1 (2004): 17–30.

17 Allen, "The Whereabouts of Power," 83.

18 Allen, "The Whereabouts of Power," 86.

19 Maarten van Aalst, Terry Cannon, and Ian Burton, "Community Level Adaptation to Climate Change: The Potential Role of Participatory Community Risk Assessment," *Global Environmental Change* 18, no. 1 (2008): 165–79.

20 Van Aalst *et al.*, "Community Level Adaptation to Climate Change," 166.

21 Van Aalst *et al.*, "Community Level Adaptation to Climate Change," 168.

22 Van Aalst *et al.*, "Community Level Adaptation to Climate Change," 179.

23 Allen, "The Whereabouts of Power," 94.

24 Shove, "Beyond the ABC."

25 Peter Miller and Nikolas Rose, "Governing Economic Life," *Economy and Society* 19, no. 1 (1990): 8; Jennifer A. Summerville, Barbara A. Adkins, and Gavin Kendall, "Community Participation, Rights, and Responsibilities: The Governmentality of Sustainable Development Policy in Australia," *Environment and Planning C: Government and Policy* 26, no. 4 (2008): 697.

26 Summerville *et al.*, "Community Participation, Rights, and Responsibilities," 697.

27 Emily Boyd, Maria Gutierrez, and Manyu Chang, "Small-scale Forest Carbon Projects: Adapting CDM to Low Income Communities," *Global Environmental Change* 17, no. 2 (2007): 250–9.

28 Gordon Walker, Sue Hunter, Patrick Devine-Wright, Bob Evans, and Helen Fay, "Harnessing Community Energies: Explaining and Evaluating Community-based Localism in Renewable Energy Policy in the UK," *Global Environmental Politics* 7, no. 2 (2007): 64–82.

29 William M. Adams, *Green Development: Environment and Sustainability in the South* (London: Routledge, 2001).

30 William Adams and Jon Hutton, "People, Parks and Poverty: Political Ecology and Biodiversity Conservation," *Conservation and Society* 5, no. 2 (2007): 147–83; Peter Sand, "Fortress Conservation Trumps Human Rights? The "Marine Protected Area" in the Chagos Archipelago," *Journal of Environment and Development* 21, no. 1 (2012): 36–40.

31 Boyd *et al.*, "Small-scale Forest Carbon Projects," 251.

32 Boyd *et al.*, "Small-scale Forest Carbon Projects," 251.

33 Adam Bumpus and Diana Liverman, "Accumulation by Decarbonisation and the Governance of Carbon Offsets," *Economic Geography* 84, no. 2 (2008): 127–56; Centre on Energy Climate and Sustainable Development, "CDM Projects by

Type" (2014), available online at http://cdmpipeline.org/cdm-projects-type.htm [accessed January 21, 2015]; In 2007, 18 percent of projects in the voluntary market were made up of forestry projects, while in 2012, the voluntary sector drove 95 percent of forestry carbon markets. See Katherine Hamilton, Milo Sjardin, Thomas Marcello, and Gordon Xu Forging, "A Frontier: State of the Voluntary Carbon Markets," in *Ecosystem Marketplace and New Carbon Finance* (2008), available online at http://www.ecosystemmarketplace.com/documents/cms_documents/2008_StateofVoluntaryCarbonMarket2.pdf [accessed January 21, 2015]; Molly Peters-Stanley, Gloria Gonzalez, and Daphne Yin, *Covering New Ground: State of the Carbon Forest Markets 2013* (2013), available online at http://www.forest-trends.org/documents/files/SOFCM-full-report.pdf [accessed January 21, 2015].

34 "REDD+" refers to measures that go beyond measures seeking to reduce deforestation and forest degradation to include "the role of conservation, sustainable management of forests and enhancement of forest carbon stocks."

35 Boyd *et al.*, "Small-scale Forest Carbon Projects," 254.

36 Esteve Corbera, Carmen González Soberanis, and Katrina Brown, "Institutional Dimensions of Payments for Ecosystem Services: An Analysis of Mexico's Carbon Forestry Programme," *Ecological Economics* 68, no. 3 (2009): 743–61.

37 Corbera *et al.*, "Institutional Dimensions of Payments for Ecosystem Services."

38 Corbera *et al.*, "Institutional Dimensions of Payments for Ecosystem Services," 751.

39 Corbera *et al.*, "Institutional Dimensions of Payments for Ecosystem Services," 751.

40 Corbera *et al.*, "Institutional Dimensions of Payments for Ecosystem Services," 755.

41 Steffen Böhm and Saddhartha Dabhi, eds, *Upsetting the Offset: The Political Economy of Carbon Markets* (Colchester: MayFly Books, 2009); Peter Newell and Adam Bumpus, "The Global Political Ecology of the CDM," *Global Environmental Politics* 12, no. 4: 49–68.

42 Bumpus and Liverman, "Accumulation by Decarbonisation and the Governance of Carbon Offsets."

43 Bumpus and Liverman, "Accumulation by Decarbonisation and the Governance of Carbon Offsets."

44 Steve Ball and Jaspar Makala, "Making REDD+ Work for Forests and Communities: Three Shared Lessons for Project Designers," *Gatekeeper No. 155* (London: IIED, 2013), available online at http://pubs.iied.org/pdfs/17211IIED.pdf [accessed January 21, 2015].

45 Kathleen Lawlor, Erin Myers Madeira, Jill Blockhus, and David J. Ganz, "Community Participation and Benefits in REDD+: A Review of Initial Outcomes and Lessons," *Forests* 4, no. 2 (2013): 296–318.

46 Walker *et al.*, "Harnessing Community Energies," 65.

47 Walker *et al.*, "Harnessing Community Energies," 70.

48 Gordon Walker, "What are the Barriers and Incentives for Community-owned Means of Energy Production and Use," *Energy Policy* 36, no. 12 (2008): 4401–5.

49 Baywind Energy, Homepage available online at www.baywind.co.uk [accessed January 21, 2015].

50 Walker, "What are the Barriers and Incentives for Community-owned Means of Energy Production and Use," 4401.
51 Gordon Walker and Patrick Devine-Wright, "Community Renewable Energy: What Should it Mean?" *Energy Policy* 36, no. 2 (2008): 498–9.
52 Walker *et al.*, "Harnessing Community Energies," 71–3.
53 John Barry, Geraint Ellis, and Clive Robinson, "Cool Rationalities and Hot Air: A Rhetorical Approach to Understanding Debates on Renewable Energy," *Global Environmental Politics* 8, no. 2 (2008): 67–98.
54 Walker *et al.*, "Harnessing Community Energies," 73.
55 *The Guardian*, "Solar Subsidies to be Cut by Half," Monday October 31, 2011, available online at www.theguardian.com/environment/2011/oct/28/solar-subsidies-cut-half [accessed January 21, 2015].
56 Energy Saving Trust, "Feed-In Tariffs scheme (FITs)", available online at www.energysavingtrust.org.uk/Generating-energy/Getting-money-back/Feed-In-Tariffs-scheme-FITs [accessed January 21, 2015].
57 Low Carbon West Oxford, Homepage, available online at www.lowcarbon-westoxford.org.uk/the-west-oxford-model [accessed January 21, 2015].
58 Sarah Irving, "Transitional Demands," *Red Pepper*, December 2009, available online at www.redpepper.org.uk/Transitional-demands/ [accessed January 21, 2015].
59 Rob Hopkins and Peter Lipman, "The Transition Network Ltd: Who We Are and What We Do . . .," available online at http://transitionculture.org/wp-content/uploads/who_we_are_high.pdf [accessed January 21, 2015]; Transition Network, *Transition Initiatives Map*, available online at www.tran-sitionnetwork.org/initiatives/map [accessed January 21, 2015].
60 Kelvin Mason and Mark Whitehead, "Transition Urbanism and the Contested Politics of Spatial Practice," *Annual International Conference of the Royal Geographical Society with the Institute of British Geographers*, 2008; see also Transition Network, *Becoming Official*, available online at www.transition-network.org/support/becoming-official [accessed January 21, 2015].
61 Mason and Whitehead, "Transition Urbanism and the Contested Politics of Spatial Practice," 8.
62 Transition Town Totnes, *Food Group Homepage*, available online at http://totnes.transitionnetwork.org/food/home [accessed January 21, 2015].
63 Transition Town Brixton, *Food and Growing Group*, available online at www.transitiontownbrixton.org/groups-and-projects/foodgrowing-group/ [accessed January 21, 2015].
64 Sustainable Berea, *Resilient Household*, available online at http://sustainable-berea.org/projects/the-resilient-household/ [accessed January 21, 2015].
65 Gill Seyfang, Sabine Hielscher, Tom Hargreaves, Mari Martiskainen, and Adrian Smith, "A Grassroots Sustainable Energy Niche? Reflections on Community Energy in the UK," *Environmental Innovation and Societal Transitions*, doi: 10.1016/j.eist.2014.04.004; Adrian Smith and Adrian Ely, "Green Transformations from Below? The Politics of Grassroots Innovation," in *The Politics of Green Transformation,* eds Ian Scoones, Melissa Leach, and Peter Newell (Abingdon: Routledge, 2015).
66 "Getting Beyond the Climate Crunch: Re-thinking Rights, Risks and Responsibilities," *ESRC Briefing* (2014), available online at http://www.lwec.org.uk/sites/default/files/attachments_site_section/Concept%20note_0.pdf [accessed January 21, 2015].

5

THE PRIVATE GOVERNANCE OF CLIMATE CHANGE

In this chapter, we focus on the increasingly important role of the private sector in the governance of climate change. As market and political actors in their own right, private sector organizations, and key industries in the energy and transport sectors in particular, have played a significant role in the evolution of the climate regime: providing expertise, lobbying governments and international institutions, and traditionally cautioning against strident action on the issue. More recently, however, many firms have come to see action on climate change as a potential opportunity rather than a threat. From emissions trading to the carbon offset market, from investments in technology to the use of a range of corporate social responsibility tools and investment strategies, financial and business actors now play a central role in the day-to-day governance of climate change. We explore how, as well as influencing traditional forms of state-led international governance, private actors have increasingly been constructing their own forms of governance, and the challenges this creates.

Business and climate change

It is difficult to overstate the importance of the private sector in proposals to address climate change. A significant proportion of the world's GHG emissions can be attributed directly or indirectly to corporations (see Introduction).[1] As the Business Council for Sustainable Development acknowledged at the time the UNFCCC was negotiated in 1992, "Industry accounts for more than one third of energy consumed world wide and uses more energy than any other end-user in industrialized and newly industrializing economies."[2] To reinforce the point, Greenpeace International showed some years later, in a comparison of CO_2 emissions from the burning of fossil fuels by major oil companies with country emissions from fossil fuel combustion, that Shell emits more than Saudi Arabia, Amoco more than Canada, Mobil more than Australia, and BP, Exxon, and Texaco more than France, Spain, and the Netherlands.[3] At the same time, the UN estimated that 86 percent of global investment and financial flows required to tackle climate change will need to come from the private sector.[4] It is not just their contribution to the problem and role in funding solutions, however, which makes business such as key actor. As the International Chamber of Commerce put it:

> Industry's involvement is a critical factor in the policy deliberations relating to climate change. It is industry that will meet the growing demands of consumers for goods and services. It is industry that develops and disseminates most of the world's technology. It is industry and the private financial community that marshal most of the financial resources that fund the world's economic growth. It is industry that develops, finances, and manages most of the investments that enhance and protect the environment. It is industry, therefore, that will be called upon to implement and finance a substantial part of governments' climate change policies.[5]

Business has hence been cast simultaneously as the problem and the source of solutions to climate change. Simply put, it is perhaps truer now than ever that constructive business engagement with the climate issue is a precondition to effective action since much of the control of production, technology, and finance that is driving climate change and that needs to be de-carbonized lies in private hands.[6] Responses to climate change that fail to account for the activities of transnational business in particular will likely preclude effective and equitable solutions to the issue.[7]

Shaping the climate regime

For a long time, businesses mobilized themselves to stall action on climate change. Climate change first registered on the radar screen of fossil fuel firms in the late 1980s and early 1990s amid growing demands for an international treaty to address the issue. The IPCC had been set up in 1988 and negotiations were set in train through the Intergovernmental Negotiating Committee for a UNFCCC (as we saw in Chapter 1). It was at this moment that businesses, whose interests were threatened by the prospect of action to reduce the use of fossil fuels, began to organize themselves politically. They moved into gear to hire lobbyists and form coalitions to present and advance their interests.

Two in particular stood out at this time; the Global Climate Coalition (GCC) and the Climate Council. Members included all the main oil companies, car manufacturers, steel firms, US electricity generators, as well as associations like the US National Association of Manufacturers and the National Mining Association.[8] Though now disbanded, it is difficult to overestimate the importance of the GCC during the early to mid-1990s as the dominant voice of concerned industry in the international climate negotiations. As Robert Reinstein, former head of the US climate delegation, and industry lobbyist at the time, told us back in 1996, "when GCC, which represents companies constituting a very significant proportion of the country's GDP start making noises, they obviously get attention."[9] At the national level, groups such as the Confederation of British Industry (United Kingdom), the World Coal Institute (World Coal Association since 2010) (UK), the American Petroleum Institute or Western Fuels Association (United States), as well as regional groupings such as employers' organizations (Union of Industrial Employers' Confederations in Europe, UNICE) (now Business Europe) and business round tables such as the European Round Table of Industrialists (ERT), sought to fight off policy measures that threatened their interests. One such measure was the EU carbon tax proposed in 1992 which, according to *The Economist*, "spurred the massed ranks of Europe's industrialists to mount what is probably their most powerful offensive against an EC (European Council) proposal."[10] Shocked at the intensity of business mobilization against the tax, Carlo Ripa di Meana, EU Environment Commissioner at the time, described the lobbying offensive as a "violent assault."[11]

A multipronged political strategy was developed to promote the voice of industry in climate debates cautioning against hasty action. First, groups sought to challenge the science behind climate change. Scientists such as Fred Singer, Robert Balling, and Patrick Michaels, skeptics of the prevailing consensus on climate change, were provided with funds from fossil fuel companies to support their research which raised questions about human contributions to climate change. Such a strategy was successful in part because the fossil fuel lobby was (and in many ways still is) so well linked to those governments that contribute most to global warming. In the United States, Chief of Staff John Sununu, a well-known climate change skeptic, played a key part in ensuring that President Bush Snr. was exposed only to doubts about the science and studies that emphasized the costs of taking action. Sununu's director of communications in the White House was John Schlaes who went on to head the Global Climate Coalition leading the business challenge to a treaty on climate change. Insiders such as Sununu certainly made the job of industry lobbyists a whole lot easier. Today, climate skeptic organizations such as the Global Warming Foundation, led by the former Chancellor of the Exchequer in the United Kingdom, Nigel Lawson, still manage to achieve disproportionately high levels of media exposure by continuing to raise questions about the extent and severity of climate change and therefore whether mitigation actions are justifiable, as well as maintain close links with key politicians such as the (former) UK Environment Minister Owen Paterson.[12]

Second, as the links between climate skeptics and their industry backers became more public, another strategy started to appeal to those businesses opposing action. Recognizing that skeptical publics were more likely to trust NGOs over government and business in environmental debates, the idea was to create business-funded environmental NGOs or what many critics call "astroturf" organizations.[13] Their role was to persuade an increasingly anxious public that fears about climate change were misplaced and to emphasize the crucial role of fossil fuels in economic development. In one case, the Western Fuels Association, the Edison Electric Institute, and the National Coal Association of the United States created the benign sounding Information Council for the Environment, which launched a US$500,000 advertising campaign "to reposition global warming as theory, not fact."[14] This sum was more than the combined amount spent by the Environmental Defense Fund, the Sierra Club, Natural Resources Defense Fund, World Wide Fund for Nature (WWF), and the Union of Concerned Scientists on their climate campaigns. Other examples included the Coalition for Vehicle Choice, a corporate front organization who ran an infamous campaign with a woman complaining that "the government wants to take away my SUV."[15] In the run-up to Kyoto, these groups spent US$13 million in an advertising campaign designed to discredit both the Kyoto Protocol in particular, and fears about climate change more generally.

The third element of the strategy was to emphasize the economic costs of tackling climate change. The fossil fuel lobby set to work producing economic studies suggesting that economies would be driven into recession if they adopted measures proposed by leading scientists. The Australian Bureau of Agriculture and Resource Economics (ABARE), for example, conducted a series of modeling exercises that predicted the loss of jobs and income if emission reduction targets were accepted. The membership of the group's steering committee included Mobil, Exxon (now ExxonMobil), Texaco, and Statoil. Publicity material published by ABARE made clear why participation at a cost of AU$50,000 was a good deal: "by becoming a member . . . you will have influence on the direction of the model development."[16] While the modeling activities of ABARE were submitted for investigation by the

Australian Conservation Foundation to the Commonwealth Ombudsman and found to be open to accusations of exclusivity and bias, the key message that acting on climate change would have significant economic costs had a direct bearing on the position adopted by the Australian Government during the international negotiations.[17]

Related to concerns about the economics of addressing climate change was the argument that if emissions were only reduced in the North, businesses would merely relocate the most polluting parts of their business overseas, producing a loss of competitiveness and no net gains in emission reductions. In a globalized economy of capital mobility and internationalized structures of production, it was argued, there is no point in one country taking action if others do not do the same. This has become known as the problem of "carbon leakage." This led to the adoption of a fourth strategy: double-edged diplomacy aimed at creating stalemate in the negotiations towards a deal on Kyoto. For example, while former chief executive of Exxon Lee Raymond was busy arguing in the United States that no action should be taken there unless China, India, and other developing countries also undertook actions, in front of audiences in China, party leaders and their industries were encouraged to resist calls from the United States to take action on climate change since this was a problem that China had contributed very little to. Using domestic politics to stall international progress on a deal was the fifth tactic in the armory of those firms intent on stalling the development of the climate regime. Press conferences at the climate negotiations were used to parade petitions from US senators promising to veto any Kyoto deal that did not include emission reduction targets for developing countries. This demand came from the Byrd–Hagel resolution passed in 1997 (see Chapter 1) which made US support for Kyoto conditional on developing countries accepting binding emission reduction obligations, which was a distant prospect at the time. This effectively tied the hands of President Clinton's negotiators since the Senate has to ratify by two-thirds any treaty that the government signs up to.

Each of these strategies fed into the sixth pillar of firms' political strategy at the time, directly influencing the climate change negotiations. Groups such as the Global Climate Coalition and the Climate Council, and in particular their respective heads John Schlaes and Don Pearlman, worked closely with oil exporting states whose interests were also threatened by the prospect of emission cuts. From drafting paragraphs of text that delegations would then introduce as their own into draft UN treaty text (often even left in Pearlman's handwriting) to hosting press conferences warning of the calamitous consequences of taking action on climate change, the fossil fuel industries managed to gain an important hold over the emerging climate regime. For example, a proposal submitted by Saudi Arabia in 1994 that protocols to the convention should be adopted by three-quarters of the parties instead of the existing two-thirds, was widely attributed to John Schlaes and Don Pearlman, while the World Coal Institute, alongside OPEC and Australia, was instrumental in ensuring that implementation of the UNFCCC would be done in such a way that account is taken of the impacts on developing countries whose economies are "highly dependent on income generated from the production, processing and export and/or consumption of fossil fuels and associated energy-intensive products."[18] When their interventions and presence on the floor of the UN negotiating halls went beyond a level that was considered acceptable for groups that were officially classified as "observers" of the process, a ban on non-governmental representatives from being present on the floor of the main plenary was introduced, given that these were after all meant to be primarily intergovernmental negotiations.

Business lobbying continues in both open and more subtle ways as nuclear, gas, fracking, carbon capture and storage, and renewable industries seek to present their sectors as vital to collective efforts to address climate change and deserving of their support, even if the presence of powerful fossil fuel companies opposing action has waned somewhat.

Private governance

From a long history of opposition to action on climate change, described above, climate change has been repositioned by some elements within the business sector as a business opportunity which has led to more positive engagement with climate governance initiatives, especially in the wake of the Kyoto Protocol in 1997. Driven either by the growing sense of inevitability of action on climate change and the reputational risks of being seen to oppose it, or in many cases by perceptions of first-mover advantages and market openings that moves to de-carbonize the economy might bring, leading companies started to drop their blanket opposition to action and over time even issued collective calls for more ambitious emission reduction targets.[19]

In this new era, and beyond attempts to influence the international climate regime, we have witnessed the emergence of what is sometimes referred to as private governance in the climate change domain.[20] Private governance can take several forms, and operate either transnationally—as we saw in Chapter 3—or within national or local territories. One type of private governance involves internal processes of self-regulation—the voluntary actions of firms in reducing their own emissions. A second involves new forms of private regulation through codes of conduct, standards, reporting, and forms of certification, usually in conjunction with other non-state actors, to regulate emissions of GHG from business activities and to address concerns about the credibility of voluntary carbon markets. This includes efforts to improve performance evaluation and forms of civil regulation whose aim is to hold business to account. Here we look at examples of each in turn.

Self-regulation

The emergence of a positive approach to addressing climate change amongst some in the business sector in part reflects growing public concern with the issue and the rise of climate change as a corporate social responsibility (CSR) issue as well as a growing recognition of the economic possibilities heralded by low carbon technologies and new carbon markets. A number of NGOs, such as the Climate Group in the United Kingdom and the Pew Centre in the United States, have played an important role in this respect in making the business case for action on climate change and publicizing the benefits achieved by existing leaders in the field.

The extent to which businesses have adopted a positive approach to climate change depends on the region and firm in question.[21] There is, nevertheless, already a great deal of evidence of companies taking voluntary action on climate change to reduce their own emissions, capitalizing on the economic savings to be made and the public relations credit to be earned from being seen to take a lead on the issue. Examples of this type of voluntary governance or self-regulation include chemicals giant Du Pont, which reduced its emissions by 65 percent below their 1990 level, while IBM has saved US$115 million since 1998 through cutting its emissions. Meanwhile, in 2005, General Electric announced Ecomagination, an initiative that would see the company double investment in research for cleaner technologies to US$1.5 billion a year by 2010, double sales of environmentally friendly products to at least US$20 billion by 2010, and reduce GHG emissions by 1 percent by 2012 (from 2004 levels). The company is being rewarded financially, with revenues from the company's portfolio of energy efficient and environmentally advantageous products and services exceeding US$12 billion in 2006, up 20 percent from 2005, while the order backlog rose to US$50 billion.[22] Some firms, such as BP and Shell, have gone so far as to establish their own intra-firm trading systems which encourage competitive reductions between different parts of the firm. This carries benefits such as saving money through reduced use of energy and first-mover advantages that come from developing new technologies and production processes to meet the targets. They also represent interesting governance initiatives in their own right, emerging as they did ahead of even the European Union's own emissions trading scheme.

In this context of a growing interest in self-regulation, many firms have even come out in favor of a binding regulatory framework to lay out clear and strict emissions commitments for the immediate and long term future— in part to protect the competitive advantages that so-called first-movers on GHG emission reductions might achieve. At the time of the Bali summit in 2008, an impressive group of 150 of some of the world's best known companies (including Volkswagen, Shell, Nokia, Kodak, Philips, HSBC, General Electric, Nestlé, Adidas, Nike, Rolls Royce, Dupont, Johnson & Johnson), published a "Communiqué on Climate Change" in the *Financial Times* calling for "a comprehensive, legally binding United Nations agreement to tackle Climate Change," which included the following statement:

> The shift to a low carbon economy will create significant business opportunities. New markets for low carbon technologies and products worth billions of dollars will be created if the world acts on the scale required. In summary, we believe that tackling climate change is the pro-growth strategy. Ignoring it will ultimately undermine economic growth.[23]

In another example of anticipatory action and leadership preempting government regulation about corporate reporting of GHG emissions, many companies voluntarily release such information. In the UK context, for example, one report found that of a sample of 100 UK-listed companies, 57 percent reported carbon emissions "to some degree," while 37 percent reported numerical data on their carbon footprint. However, only 20 percent formally reported a specific target in relation to carbon reduction, only 9 percent disclosed that information on carbon had been reported in line with government guidance, and only 8 percent stated that their reported information had been assured by a third party.[24] Self-regulation and voluntary measures are not only unevenly adopted across regions and sectors, therefore, but also within the same national context.

Private regulation

Beyond the sphere of voluntary action on climate change, many corporations have also sought to construct their own standards and forms of private regulation. This serves to generate consumer and investor confidence that common and agreed standards of conduct are being adhered to. It can also reduce transaction costs (so that each firm or sector does not have to develop its own standards) and creates a more visible and institutionalized marker of commitment which has the added advantage of dissipating demands for stronger forms of public regulation from the state for some businesses.

For example, in response to concerns about the credibility of projects and credits traded in voluntary carbon markets and the extent to which they genuinely deliver social and environmental benefits (which many firms purchase in order to claim the carbon neutrality of their operations), businesses have sought to set up their own forms of standards and voluntary regulation. They allow firms to show that they are compliant with certain performance criteria. Examples include the CDM Gold Standard, the Voluntary Carbon Standard, and the Climate, Community, and Biodiversity (CCB) standard. They are significant in governance terms because of the steering roles they perform, and the informal forms of regulation and standard-setting they generate. A number of these standards claim to have at least as stringent criteria for measuring additionality as compliance markets such as the CDM. The Gold Standard, initiated by WWF International, Helio International, and South South North in 2003, includes among its objectives helping to boost investment in sustainable energy projects and increasing public support for renewable energy and energy efficiency.[25] The Gold Standard essentially applies an extra set of screens to CDM or voluntary projects using strict additionality criteria and certifying with Gold Standard credits only projects in the areas of renewable and energy efficiency and methane capture and use. To ensure sustainable development, it also places emphasis on local stakeholder consultation prior to implementation. The "boutique credits"[26] that result from these extra transaction costs are generally sold at about 25 percent above the market value for normal CERs. In many ways then it is a "beyond compliance" initiative, as it is designed to help the CDM realize its objectives and is fully integrated with CDM procedures so, for example, verifiers (Designated Operational Entities) will validate both standard CDM and Gold Standard requirements at the same time.

The Verified Carbon Standard (VCS), developed by the Climate Group, the IETA, and the WBCSD in 2006, seeks to provide a "robust global standard, program framework and institutional structure for validation and verification of voluntary GHG emission reductions."[27] It aims to "experiment and stimulate innovation in GHG mitigation technologies, verification and registration processes that can be built into other programs and regulations."[28] Part of this involves performing key governance functions such as guarding against double-counting of the same emission reductions and providing transparency for the public. The VCS Board comprises nine members from across the public and private sectors including the World Economic Forum, IETA, and International Institute for Environment and Development (IIED) while its steering committee is made up of many of the key actors in this area, including Det Norske Veritas (DNV), Ecosecurities, and Cantor CO2e. By providing rules for certification that are claimed to be as robust as those of the Kyoto Protocol's CDM, the VCS aims to give confidence to buyers and sellers. As the Climate Group put it, it does this by providing a "set of criteria that will provide integrity to the voluntary carbon market."[29] Two recent reports have found that the VCS is already the most popular standard for voluntary offset projects,[30] is leading the way by being the first carbon standard to cover all major land-use activities (whether forestry or agriculture), and that it addresses many of the "permanence and additionality" concerns that have held back the take up of projects in global carbon markets.[31]

Besides issues of environmental integrity, some standards address the social dimensions of voluntary projects. The CCB standards,[32] for example, released in 2005, aim to "identify land-based carbon projects that deliver robust GHG reductions while also delivering net positive benefits to local communities and biodiversity."[33] These provide gold, silver and standard certification for projects depending on how many of their criteria are satisfied. They range from required criteria, which include additionality, baseline issues, and leakage assessment, through to extras such as employing stakeholders in project management, worker safety, and adaptive management. Given the fatigue about the proliferation in voluntary standards, one thing CCB does is build on the use of existing certifiers, authorized under Kyoto or by the Forestry Stewardship Council for example, as third party evaluators of whether a project deserves to be certified. Most recently, in 2014, Fairtrade International and The Gold Standard Foundation joined forces to sign a collaborative agreement to develop a joint Gold Standard and Fairtrade carbon scheme to foster wider sustainable development and provide greater access to the carbon market for smallholders and rural communities in developing countries. The Fairtrade Carbon Credit standard:

> aims to enable greater access and participation in the carbon market for the most disadvantaged communities and to drive a greater proportion of carbon income to them. It will provide producers with a new climate change mitigation opportunity and help them generate additional revenue through the selling of Fairtrade Carbon Credits in the voluntary carbon market.[34]

Other initiatives that fall under the heading of private governance and which use forms of certification and benchmarking are about promoting the transparency and accountability of investors. By recording, evaluating, and comparing performance they may also, however, create pressures for firms to reduce their emissions through their investments. The Carbon Disclosure Project (CDP), for example, by systematizing information about investors' emissions, creates the means to pressure firms to invest in renewable rather than fossil fuel energy solutions. The CDP covers 767 institutional investors holding US$92 trillion in assets and thousands of companies to help reveal the risk in their investment portfolios. The scope of private regulation is, therefore, impressive and reaches key actors not subject to other forms of governance.

In a similar vein, the Greenhouse Gas Protocol (GHG Protocol) is a corporate reporting and accounting standard, jointly created by the World Resources Institute (WRI) and the WBCSD in 1998, and now claims to be "the most widely used international accounting tool for government and business leaders to understand, quantify, and manage greenhouse gas emissions."[35] Emphasizing the links between formal and informal regulation, in 2006, the International Organization for Standardization (ISO) adopted the Corporate Standard as the basis for its ISO 14064-I: Specification with Guidance at the Organization Level for Quantification and Reporting of Greenhouse Gas Emissions and Removals. On December 3, 2007, ISO, WBCSD, and WRI signed a Memorandum of Understanding to jointly promote both global standards.[36] Organizations such as the Carbon Fund meanwhile aim at "increasing awareness of products and companies that are compensating for their carbon footprint while helping to hasten a market transformation."[37] Indeed, tools such as the Carbon Fund's "Carbon Footprint Protocol" draw on guidelines and standards that govern the compliance market such as rules for CDM and Land Use, Land-Use Change and Forestry (LULUCF), since essentially they are wrestling with the same issues of proving additionality and using valid baselines.

As with all forms of climate governance, private climate governance has been contested by other actors—disputing the claims companies have made about their performance, raising concerns about the adequacy of voluntary regulation of voluntary markets, and seeking to develop tools and strategies of accountability. Such strategies are sometimes referred to as civil regulation: civil society-based regulation of the private sector.[38] Civil regulation includes the use of shareholder activism, consumer boycotts, and exposé campaigns.[39] Alternative systems of sanctions to penalize irresponsible conduct and reward positive behavior include loss of market value or consumer confidence, tarnished public reputation, and disaffection among shareholders that serve to "harden the environmental accountability demands leveled at corporations."[40] Not only do they provide "an instrument of accountability for ecological performance," but also a critical dimension of their effectiveness derives from the construction of these mechanisms of civil redress.[41] Corporations are, through these means, subject to a variety of accountability sanctions that go beyond the strict public regulation of their activities.

To take one example, many leading firms have been subject to shareholder activism. The year 2005 saw a record number of shareholder resolutions on global warming. State and city pension funds, labor foundations, and religious and other institutional shareholders filed 30 global warming resolutions requesting financial risk and disclosure plans to reduce GHG emissions. This is three times the number for 2000/01. Firms affected include leading players from the automobile sector such as Ford and General Motors; Chevron Texaco, Unocal, and ExxonMobil from the oil sector; Dow Chemicals; and market leaders in financial services such as J. P. Morgan Chase. Groups such as CERES (Coalition for Environmentally Responsible Economies) and ICCR (Interfaith Centre for Corporate Responsibility), a coalition of 275 faith-based institutional investors, have been using their financial muscle to hold firms to account for their performance on climate change. They demand both information disclosure and management practices that reflect the values of their shareholders. Overall, the resolutions led to distinctive agreements, but with some common links: acknowledging climate change impacts in securities filings and on corporate websites; assigning board-level responsibility for overseeing climate change mitigation strategy; and benchmarking and GHG emission reduction goals.[42] That many firms are now engaging with the CDP as a means of making their climate-related activities transparent may reflect the increasing pressure that such forms of civil regulation is bringing to bear.

Disclosure is the first and necessary step to applying and enforcing pressure on corporations to disinvest in fossil fuels and activists have increasingly targeted the power and vulnerability of banks, trying to persuade them that investments in fossil fuels should increasingly be seen as liabilities rather than assets, or as "stranded assets." If governments are serious about meeting climate mitigation goals, they argue, many existing investments are in "unburnable carbon" that will have to be left in the ground.[43] There is growing evidence of successful disinvestment or divestment campaigns targeted at governments, corporations and universities. To date, 22 cities, 2 counties, 20 religious organizations, 9 colleges and universities and 6 other institutions have signed up to rid themselves of investments in fossil fuel companies and Norway's US$815 billion sovereign wealth fund—the world's largest—has already halved its exposure to coal producers. In addition to these divestment announcements, many major banks and financial institutions have limited or halted their lending to coal projects.[44]

What the examples above reveal is an interesting dynamic whereby "resistance makes markets"[45] in which civil society organizations create a legitimacy crisis for corporations around their contribution to climate change. Corporations then respond by developing systems of private regulation, oftentimes working in collaboration with their NGO critics. Weaknesses in these initiatives then lead to further pressure to strengthen systems of private governance to cover more issues, more regions or reach further down the supply chain, changing business performance and the expectations surrounding it.

Governance issues and challenges

What we can see from the above examples is that the role of business in climate governance covers a wide-ranging tapestry of governance practices taking uneven forms across scales and regions. This is perhaps inevitable given the range of actors whose behavior climate governance seeks to address, but it does draw our attention to a number of critical features of the climate governance landscape.

One key feature that emerges from this chapter is the continued importance of the relation between forms of "public" and "private" governance. As we saw in the history of business involvement in the climate change negotiations, private actors have had a profound influence on the nature of public climate governance. But the reverse is also true. As is clear from the development of both market and voluntary approaches to governing climate change, the state continues to play a significant role in shaping private climate governance. Abyd Karmali, managing director and global head of carbon markets at Merrill Lynch puts it succinctly:

> Those who assume that the carbon market is purely a private market miss the point that the entire market is a creation of government policy. Moreover, it is important to realize that, to flourish, carbon markets need a strong regulator and approach to governance. This means, for example, that the emission reduction targets must be ratcheted down over time, rules about eligibility of carbon credits must be clear etc. Also, carbon markets need to work in concert with other policies and

measures since not even the most ardent market proponents are under any illusion that markets alone will solve the problem.[46]

We are witnessing the continuation of a dynamic whereby innovative forms of private governance either respond to the limits of public regulation or strive to meet a market niche in doing so, such as the Gold Standard, or seek to anticipate and preempt further public regulation which may be less sensitive to their interests such as in the case of the VCS. In short, the shadow of regulation looms large for some private sector actors as an incentive to get their own house in order before governments threaten to do it for them. For the shadow of regulation to be effective as a driver of more ambitious voluntary action, public actors have to demonstrate that they will regulate where voluntary approaches have failed. The European Union did this when it abandoned a strategy for reducing CO_2 emissions from cars based on voluntary commitments by the car industry. Under the voluntary commitments, European manufacturers had pledged to reduce emissions from their new cars to an average of 140 g/km of CO_2 by 2008. However, the Commission's review of the strategy concluded that the voluntary commitments had not succeeded and that the 140 g/km target would not be met on time without further measures. Hence it proposed a legislative framework to reduce CO_2 emissions from new cars and vans.[47]

Despite this "shadow of hierarchy," a second feature of the emergence of private forms of governance has been the breadth and scope of initiatives that are underway, often going beyond standards required in international and national policy. A positive reading of this new landscape of private regulation is that it goes further and faster than state-based action on climate change and creates new channels of pressures on key contributors to climate change.[48] With the rise of CSR and voluntary regulation, social expectations about the responsibilities of firms sometimes far outstrip those that are expressed in legal instruments, where there remains an imbalance between the rights and responsibilities of firms as they are constituted at the global level.[49] Voluntary standards are also quicker to approve, respond to private and consumer needs, and potentially provide wide coverage if adopted by large firms with extensive supply chain networks.[50] When a company like the supermarket giant Tesco in the United Kingdom announces its intention to ultimately label all the products it sells in its supermarkets according to their carbon footprint, the global reach of the measure is significant. A further contribution private governance can make is to improve and systematize levels of reporting and disclosure about GHG emissions which in itself is a form of governance and may support other standards or forms of regulation. Beyond serving as a source of credible information on GHG offsets, for example, the Offset Quality Initiative, founded in 2007 by six non-profit actors (including the Climate Trust, Pew Centre on Global Climate Change, and the Climate Group), seeks to advance the integration of key principles on carbon offset quality in emerging climate change policies at the state, regional, and federal levels.

There is a key difference, nevertheless, between state regulation of and for the private sector, and regulations established by and for private actors themselves. Voluntary regulation is discretionary and derives from incentives some leading firms have to demonstrate leadership or to seek to exploit a first-mover advantage in the market. The problem with relying on such responses is that only those firms under pressure (from within and outside the firm) and in the public spotlight will act. Given the choice, many will not, leading to problems of uneven obligations and free-riding by those that benefit from the actions taken by others without making sacrifices themselves. This is true within states and internationally, where, in the absence of global coverage, action may be ineffective if key sectors and polluters are not on board and unappealing for firms if private sectors elsewhere are not also making sacrifices, especially given the problems of "carbon leakage" described above. If we rely on making the "business case" for action on climate change, sectors that make their profits from burning fossil fuels may just not do anything.

A related concern is the issue of effectiveness. If the different mechanisms of private governance discussed here are to make a meaningful contribution to efforts to tackle climate change, they have to show that they can bring down emissions. Yet the coverage of many instruments is limited to market leaders or concentrated in particular sectors or regions. In general, it seems that companies participate more frequently in information-based climate change arrangements than in voluntary or legally binding market-based arrangements, and geographically speaking there tends to be a greater representation of European and North American transnational companies in private governance arrangements.[51] With the CDP, for example, the majority of the institutional investors are based either in Europe or North America. In their survey of corporate responses to climate change in the global South, Pulver and Benney found that with a few exceptions in rapidly emerging economies, where access to carbon markets was a driver, most private sector firms in the global South are not aware of or not concerned about climate change.[52]

Moreover, assessments of the overall effectiveness of voluntary corporate measures to address climate change raise serious cause for concern. Sullivan and Gouldson, for example, find:

that there have been significant and steady improvements in energy efficiency, but that these efficiency gains are often outstripped by the impacts of business growth. For most companies, short of a radical redesign of their business activities, or an expansion of the scope of their energy management initiatives to include their indirect emissions, total greenhouse gas emissions will tend to increase over time.[53]

Concerns remain, therefore, that while companies have shown themselves willing to take low cost actions with immediate benefits, where reducing emissions require significant capital investment and where the profitability of such investments is highly sensitive to climate change policy, many companies have opted for a "wait and see" strategy.[54]

There are also issues of process, of who participates and how, and of accountability for actions and inactions. Some forms of private governance allow for more participation, transparency and accountability than others. The CDP questionnaire and reports, for example, are public and can be accessed via the Internet. Responses from companies are available without restriction. The CDP operates on an essentially self-select basis, in so far as the initiative is voluntary. Yet the flexibility built into the CDP means that firms are able to choose which of their operations they include in their emissions disclosure. Indeed, most companies signed up to the CDP place a disclaimer that the information they enclose does not include their activities in some developing countries. Discrepancies also appear when a different emissions profile emerges from the same company reporting on the same site to two different reporting standards. Initiatives such as the Carbon Disclosure Standards Board, created in 2010, seek to address this issue by acting as a forum for collaboration on how existing standards and practices can be used to link financial and climate change-related information with its Climate Change Reporting Framework.

Nevertheless, there are often no institutional control mechanisms in place to monitor and verify company responses, though the levels of public access noted above do mean other actors are in a position, at least in theory, to challenge or investigate for themselves claims made by firms submitting data. Interestingly, bodies such as the US Financial Industry Regulatory Authority handled verification and monitoring issues for some schemes, because the organization is primarily a commodity trading body, suggesting once again that private initiatives often fall back on state authority.[55]

Thinking about private governance generates interesting theoretical as well as policy challenges, therefore. The everyday forms of governance and regulation that firms generate, often on scales and overseeing resources far greater than those over which governments have direct control, are poorly captured by traditional explanations of governance which focus on the public, the interstate, the global, and the formal. The increasing profile of business in these debates reflects not just the turn towards market-based solutions to climate change which affect and imply business involvement (as we saw in Chapter 1), but also broader shifts in power between state and market in a context of globalization. Among different sectors of business, the key role of finance in contemporary forms of neo-liberalism is particularly notable and explains the focus on carbon disclosure, efforts to woo the insurance industry, and to work with leading banks such as HSBC.[56] The forms of governance deployed—the emphasis on partnerships with civil society and other actors, voluntarism, and networks—reflect neo-liberal modes of governance. More specifically, the way firms draw boundaries around what is to be governed, how, by whom, and for whom, are very different from the way states and international institutions or cities do, for example. The ways in which they produce governance raises difficult issues of transparency, representation, and legitimacy. And yet, whether it is oil firms or banks, business actors are increasingly central to any effort to govern climate change. For all these reasons private governance forces us to think more innovatively about how and where governance happens, and who is served and who is disadvantaged by particular arrangements.

Notes

1 Rory Sullivan and Andy Gouldson, "Ten Years of Corporate Action on Climate Change: What Do We Have to Show for It?," *Energy Policy* 60 (2013): 733–40.
2 Stephen Schmidheiny and the Business Council for Sustainable Development, *Changing Course* (Boston, Mass.: MIT Press, 1992), 43.
3 Greenpeace International, "The Oil Industry and Climate Change: A Greenpeace Briefing" (Amsterdam, the Netherlands: Greenpeace International, 1998).
4 UNFCCC, "Investment and Financial Flows to Address Climate Change" (Bonn, Germany: UNFCCC, 2007).
5 International Chamber of Commerce, "Statement by the International Chamber of Commerce Before COP1," Berlin, Germany, March 29, 1995.
6 Jonathan Pinske and Ans Kolk, *International Business and Climate Change* (Abingdon: Routledge, 2009).
7 Yda Schreuder, *The Corporate Greenhouse: Climate Change Policy in a Globalizing World* (London: Zed Books, 2009).
8 David Levy, "Business and the Evolution of the Climate Regime: The Dynamics of Corporate Strategies," in *The Business of Global Environmental Governance*, eds David Levy and Peter Newell (Cambridge, Mass.: MIT Press, 2005), 73–105.

9 Cited in Peter Newell, *Climate for Change: Non-State Actors and the Global Politics of the Greenhouse* (Cambridge: Cambridge University Press, 2000), 100.

10 "Europe's Industries Play Dirty," *The Economist*, May 9, 1992.

11 Peter Newell and Mathew Paterson, "A Climate for Business: Global Warming, the State and Capital," *Review of International Political Economy* 5, no. 4 (Winter 1998): 679–704.

12 "Former Environment Secretary Owen Paterson to Deliver Keynote Speech at Climate-Sceptic Organisation's Lecture," *The Independent*, July 18, 2014, available online at www.independent.co.uk/news/uk/politics/former-environment-secretary-owen-paterson-to-deliver-keynote-speech-at-climatesceptic-organisations-lecture-9615807.html [accessed January 21, 2015].

13 Carl Deal, *The Greenpeace Guide to Anti-Environmental Organizations* (Berkeley, Calif.: Odonian Press, 1993).

14 Ross Gelbspan, *The Heat Is on: The Climate Crisis, the Cover-Up, the Prescription* (Reading, Mass.: Perseus Books Group, 1998).

15 Danny Hakim, "The Media Business: Ads are a Weapon in the Battle Over Higher Fuel Standards," *New York Times*, March 12, 2002, available online at www.nytimes.com/2002/03/12/business/media-business-advertising-ads-are-weapon-battle-over-higher-auto-fuel-standards.html?pagewanted=all [accessed January 21, 2015].

16 Newell, *Climate for Change.*

17 Harriet Bulkeley, "No Regrets? Economy and Environment in Australia's Domestic Climate Change Policy Process," *Global Environmental Change: Human and Policy Dimensions* 11, no. 2 (2001): 155–69.

18 Article 4 of the UNFCCC (1992), available online at http://unfccc.int/resource/docs/convkp/conveng.pdf [accessed January 21, 2015].

19 Kathryn Begg, Frans van der Woerd, and David Levy, eds, *The Business of Climate Change: Corporate Responses to Kyoto* (Sheffield: Greenleaf Publishing, 2005); Peter Newell and Matthew Paterson, *Climate Capitalism* (Cambridge: Cambridge University Press, 2010).

20 Robert Falkner, "Private Environmental Governance and International Relations: Exploring the Links," *Global Environmental Politics* 3, no. 2 (2003): 72–88; Philipp Pattberg, *Private Institutions and Global Governance: The New Politics of Environmental Sustainability* (Cheltenham, UK: Edward Elgar, 2007).

21 David Levy and Peter Newell, "Oceans Apart? Comparing Business Responses to the Environment in Europe and North America," *Environment* 42, no. 9 (2000): 8–20; Ian Rowlands, "Beauty and the Beast? BP's and Exxon's Positions on Global Climate Change," *Environment and Planning C: Government and Policy* 18, no. 3 (2000): 339–54; Ingvild Andreassen Sæverud and Jon Birger Skjærseth, "Oil Companies and Climate Change: Inconsistencies Between Strategy Formulation and Implementation?" *Global Environmental Politics* 7, no. 3 (2007): 42–63.

22 GE Eco-Imagination Report, *Investing and Delivering on Eco-imagination*, available online at http://ge.ecomagination.com/site/downloads/news/2007ecoreport.pdf [accessed January 21, 2015].

23 The Bali communiqué on climate change, available online at www.princeofwales.gov.uk/sites/default/files/documents/Bali%20Communique.pdf [accessed January 21, 2015].

24 *Carbon Reporting to Date: Seeing the Wood for the Trees* (London: Deloitte Touche, 2010).

25 CDM Gold Standard (2014), available online at www.goldstandard.org/ [accessed January 21, 2015].

26 Adam Bumpus and Diana Liverman, "Accumulation by Decarbonization and the Governance of Carbon Offsets," *Economic Geography* 84, no. 2 (2008): 127–55.

27 Voluntary Carbon Standard, "Voluntary Carbon Standard Program Guidelines," available online at www.v-c-s.org/sites/v-c-s.org/files/Voluntary%20 Carbon%20Standard%20Program%20Guidelines%202007_1.pdf [accessed January 21, 2015].

28 Voluntary Carbon Standard, "Voluntary Carbon Standard Program Guidelines."

29 The Climate Group, 2006. See http://www.positiveclimatecare.com/vcs.html [accessed January 21, 2015].

30 Ecosystem Marketplace and New Carbon Finance, *State of the Voluntary Carbon Market* (2007), available online at http://ecosystemmarketplace. com/documents/acrobat/StateoftheVoluntaryCarbonMarket18July_Final.pdf [January 21, 2015].

31 Anja Kollmuss, Helge Zink, and Clifford Polycarp, *Making Sense of the Voluntary Carbon Market: A Comparison of Carbon Offset Standards* (Germany: WWF, 2008).

32 The Climate, Community and Biodiversity Association, *Climate, Community and Biodiversity Project Design Standards (first edition)* (Washington, DC: The Climate, Community and Biodiversity Association, 2005), available online at www.climate-standards.org [accessed January 21, 2015].

33 E-mail received from Joanna Durbin, director, Climate, Community and Biodiversity Alliance, July 30, 2008.

34 Gold Standard, "Fairtrade Carbon Credit Standard: Second Consultation," available online at www.goldstandard.org/public-consultation-fairtrade-car-bon-credit-standard [accessed January 21, 2015].

35 The Greenhouse Gas Protocol Initiative homepage, available online at www. ghgprotocol.org/ [accessed January 21, 2015].

36 ISO, "ISO, WRI, and WBCSD announce cooperation on greenhouse gas accounting and verification" (2007), available online at www.iso.org/iso/ news.htm?refid=Ref1093 [accessed January 21, 2015].

37 Carbon Fund, "Carbon Footprint Protocol," (2008), 3, available online at www.carbonfund.org [accessed January 21, 2015].

38 Simon Zadek, *The Civil Corporation: The New Economy of Corporate Citizenship* (London: Earthscan, 2001).

39 Peter Newell, "Managing Multinationals: The Governance of Investment for the Environment," *Journal of International Development* 13, no. 7 (2001): 907–19.

40 Michael Mason, *The New Accountability: Environmental Responsibility Across Borders* (London: Earthscan, 2005): 151.

41 Mason, *The New Accountability*, 150.

42 Peter Newell, "Civil Society, Corporate Accountability and the Politics of Climate Change," *Global Environmental Politics* 8, no. 3 (2008): 124–55.

43 Carbon Tracker Homepage, available online at www.carbontracker.org [accessed January 21, 2015].

44 Ecowatch, "Divestment Goes Mainstream as Major Funds Kick the Fossil Fuel Habit," available online at www.ecowatch.com/2014/02/03/divestment-mainstream-kick-fossil-fuel-habit/ [accessed January 21, 2015].

45 Matthew Paterson, "Resistance Makes Carbon Markets," in *Upsetting the Offset: The Political Economy of Carbon Markets*, eds Steffen Böhm and Saddhartha Dabhi (Colchester: MayFlyBooks, 2009), 244–54.

46 ClimateChangeCorp, "Is Carbon Trading the Most Cost-Effective Way to Reduce Emissions?" *Climate News for Business*, available online at http://www.fern.org/es/node/5231 [accessed January 21, 2015].

47 European Commission, "Commission Plans Legislative Framework to Ensure the EU Meets Its Target for Cutting CO_2 Emissions from Cars," IP/07/155 (Brussels February 7, 2007).

48 Peter Newell, Phillip Pattberg, and Heike Schroeder, "Multi-actor Governance and the Environment," *Annual Review of Environment and Resources* 37 (2012): 365–87.

49 Newell, "Managing Multinationals," 907–19.

50 Timothy M. Smith, "Climate Change: Corporate Sustainability in the Supply Chain," *Bulletin of the Atomic Scientists* 69, no. 3 (2013): 43–52.

51 Harriet Bulkeley, Liliana Andonova, Karin Bäckstrand, Michele Betsill, Daniel Compagnon, Rosaleen Duffy, Ans Kolk, Matthew Hoffmann, David Levy, Peter Newell, Tori Milledge, Matthew Paterson, Philipp Pattberg, and Stacy VanDeveer, "Governing Climate Change Transnationally: Assessing the Evidence from a Database of Sixty Initiatives," *Environment and Planning C: Government and Policy* 30, no. 4 (2012): 591–612.

52 Simone Pulver and Tabitha Benney, "Private Sector Responses to Climate Change in the Global South," *WIRES: Climate Change* 4, no. 6 (2013): 479–96.

53 Sullivan and Gouldson, "Ten Years of Corporate Action on Climate Change," 733.

54 Chukwumerije Okereke, "An Exploration of Motivations, Drivers and Barriers To Carbon Management: The UK FTSE100," *European Management Journal* 25, no. 6 (2007), 475–86; Øyvind Ihlen, "Business and Climate Change: The Climate Response of the World's 30 Largest Corporations," *Environmental Communication: A Journal of Nature and Culture* 3, no. 2 (2009): 244–62.

55 Robert Falkner, "Private Environmental Governance and International Relations: Exploring the Links," *Global Environmental Politics* 3, no. 2 (2003): 72–88; Lars Gulbrandsen, "Accountability Arrangements in Non-State Standards Organizations: Instrumental Design and Imitation," *Organization* 15, no. 4 (2008): 563–83.

56 Peter Newell and Mathew Paterson, "The Politics of the Carbon Economy," in *The Politics of Climate Change*, ed. Max Boykoff (London: Routledge, 2009).

6

CONCLUSIONS

Once upon a time, studying and keeping track of the world of climate governance was relatively simple. By attending the UN climate change negotiations or reading *Earth Negotiations Bulletin*[1] and the NGO newsletter *ECO* you could essentially keep up to date with what was going on. If you take the view that international institutions continue to be the primary and most important site of climate governance, your task continues to be a relatively straightforward one, even if the range of issues on the negotiating table has grown more complex. If, however, you adopt a broader view of climate governance—one that takes a broader and more open view about how and where it happens and who is engaged in it—as we have done in this book, your task is altogether more complex. In this final chapter we summarize some of the key cross-cutting themes that have emerged throughout the book, what they imply for governing climate change, and how we can make sense of them.

The shifting terrain of governance

Claiming that the landscape of climate governance is more plural, diverse, and multifaceted is not to say that the governance of climate change by and through international institutions and nation-states does not continue to be a central part of the story. Key decisions about overall targets and the means of delivering them continue to be made at the international level by nation-states operating within global institutions. We saw in Chapter 1 how historical and contemporary conflicts along North–South and other lines continue to get played out in the UN negotiations through debates about responsibility for the problem and the appropriate responses to it. This includes contentious discussions about the appropriate vehicles for delivering funding, such as the ongoing debates about the governance of the Green Climate Fund as we saw in Chapter 2.

However, we have also seen examples of a tremendous proliferation in governance initiatives around the world at all scales of politics (from the local to the global) that enroll a vast array of state, non-state, public, and private actors in different dimensions of governing.[2] These have taken the form of public–private and hybrid initiatives (such as REEEP and CDM), of private codes and standard-setting (such as the VCS, Gold Standard, or GHG Protocol), or community-based initiatives such as Transition Town projects. As the dimensions of the challenge of tackling climate change become clearer and the debate moves from setting goals to implementation, it has become increasingly obvious that climate governance can no longer be achieved by the actions and initiatives of international institutions or national governments alone. Rather, the growth of new "sites" of climate politics that we have documented in this book is testament to the increasing mainstreaming of climate change—its integration into other policy domains (biodiversity, trade, energy)—and its increasing uptake by a range of organizations (be they corporate, donor, or civil society) beyond the realm of what was traditionally considered as climate governance.

We have seen, though, that with this shifting terrain come a number of critical challenges. Governing across so many scales and through so many dispersed but overlapping networks presents huge problems of coordination and policy coherence. We saw in Chapter 2 how the number of banks, donors, and NGOs clamoring to define a leading role for themselves in the delivery of carbon finance is creating problems of duplication and turf wars over who funds what. As a premium is placed on the delivery of clean energy we have seen the REEEP initiative set up, the REN21 network created, and numerous energy investments overseen by the World Bank and regional development banks in Asia and Latin America. In such a crowded field, there are challenges of ensuring a rational division of labor which allows each actor to do what it does best in terms of regional, technological, or sectoral focus.

Just as actors beyond the traditional world of climate policy are becoming increasingly involved in its governance, so too actors concerned with climate change involve themselves in the governance of other sectors, such as energy, trade, industry, agriculture, and housing, to name but a few. This creates problems of policy coherence at the national level; ensuring that actions in such areas are compatible with and do not undermine climate policy goals. But these issue linkages are also apparent at the international level in debates about the compatibility of climate policy measures with the international trade regime, for example. One potential trade conflict at the World Trade Organization (WTO) over the fairness of China's clean technology subsidies and domestic sourcing requirements (so-called import substitution subsidies), was narrowly avoided in 2011 when China agreed to end the use of the subsidies in question.[3] In 2014, the WTO also established a panel to hear a US complaint against India's National Solar Mission on the basis that India's use of local content requirements in the scheme violates WTO's subsidy rules. How this issue, and others, is resolved will be shaped by who wields most power and whose rules rule. Managing the shifting terrain and multiple sites of climate governance is not just a matter of improved coordination. The power of key actors with interests at stake will be brought to bear in determining what counts as legitimate climate governance, and how, where, and by whom particular issues such as this get resolved.

New actors, old politics?

The shifting terrain of climate governance is in part a reflection of the realization that the resources, capacity, expertise, networks, and power of actors as diverse as states, firms, cities, communities, civil society organizations, and individuals are required to effectively address all aspects of the problem. While nation-states and international institutions remain critical actors, what we have found is that the delivery of the targets and agreed commitments often implies an important role for many other actors such as businesses and cities, and in reality is dependent on their support and engagement if it is to be effective. As David Levy argues, "if an agreement cannot be crafted that gains the consent of major affected industries, there will likely be no agreement at all."[4] They are, after all, the "street level bureaucrats" that will be expected to put regulation into practice.[5] Often, however, as well as helping to realize the goals of the regime through their own independent actions, these actors are going beyond the formal climate regime by setting more ambitious targets than those contained in Kyoto. For example, the 2007 Bali World Mayors and Local Governments Climate Protection Agreement states that municipal authorities will seek to reduce GHG emissions by 60 percent worldwide by 2050, with an 80 percent reduction in emissions from industrialized countries,[6] or engage in forms of governance innovation that precede and predate those adopted by government. The oil giants Shell and BP had both developed intra-firm emissions trading schemes from 2000, for example, three years before the EU ETS was established.

The involvement of multiple actors in the governing of climate change has not been a necessarily harmonious and consensual process, however.

We have seen how actors with conflicting interests in the debate compete to assert their preferred understanding of the nature of the challenges associated with climate change. We saw in Chapter 1 how there has been fierce contestation over whether sufficient scientific consensus exists to justify potentially costly forms of action for some actors. Conflicts over which evidence is highlighted in the policymakers' summaries produced by the IPCC reflect what is at stake in the recommendations that flow from how the risks associated with acting or not acting are presented. We saw in Chapter 5 how the business community throughout much of the 1990s sought to present climate change as a threat to economic growth rather than an opportunity to develop new successful forms of low-carbon business. Battles continue today among and within firms about whether climate change is a threat or an opportunity to their business.

The issue of who governs directly impinges upon the question of who benefits from current governance arrangements. We saw in Chapter 1 that disputes over the role of the World Bank in managing the Green Climate Fund reflect developing country concerns about the Bank's responsiveness to their developmental needs and priorities. We have also seen how many smaller developing countries, those most vulnerable to the effects of climate change in many cases, are poorly represented in the international negotiations, and lack the legal and scientific capacity to engage fully in the discussions taking place. We used the example of the legal support given by the environmental legal NGO FIELD to the Alliance of Small Island States most affected by sea-level rise to bolster their negotiating capacity vis-à-vis more powerful countries and regions. At the same time, the mutual dependence of state and non-state actors in realizing climate governance goals is leading to compromises and new forms of partnership. In Chapter 4, we saw how various forms of community are being mobilized by states and international institutions in order to address climate change. This can bring benefits, both in terms of addressing climate change and for wider goals of social and environmental justice, but can also lead to the exclusion of those actors' interests and goals that do not fit with particular interpretations of the climate governance "project." Attending to the politics of who governs, and on whose behalf, will be critical to ensuring that addressing climate change does not come at a cost to those least able to represent their interests.

The rise of market and voluntary governance

Throughout the book we have also seen that who governs, and importantly how they govern, is in a continual state of flux in the world of climate politics. What is possible and likely from climate governance is a feature of the health of the economy, the nature of relations between states, and which other issues compete with climate change for resources and attention—all of which are subject to change. This broader political and economic context shapes and is shaped by climate governance. We saw in Chapter 2 how the popularity of market-based mechanisms in climate governance can best be understood within a prevailing context of neo-liberalism; an ideology and set of practices which assume a minimal role for the state and view the market as the main provider of efficient outcomes. The embrace of emissions trading and the creation of the CDM, where earlier they had been opposed, can be understood as a result of the deepening hold of neo-liberalism throughout the 1990s as well as the ability of its most powerful proponent, the United States, to insist such solutions be part of the global deal, even one they then refused to be part of! Likewise, the call for communities to govern themselves in order to address climate change, as discussed in Chapter 4, and the growth in partnership approaches, explored in Chapter 3, are also means of governing global affairs that fit with neo-liberal ideas about the respective roles of the state, of the private sector, and of individuals.[7]

The cases in this book have also demonstrated a dynamic relationship between formal and informal forms of soft regulation. The CDM Gold Standard is a private non-governmental initiative that provides "compliance plus" incentives for investments in projects that meet certain sustainable development criteria. It does not compete with the CDM rules agreed under the Kyoto Protocol, but rather provides the incentives and means for those who want to go beyond them to do so. We also saw how voluntary governance experiments, such as with forestry projects in voluntary carbon offset markets, can prepare the way for their acceptance into the formal climate regime. On the other hand, some initiatives such as the Asia–Pacific Partnership on Clean Development and Climate, initially interpreted as an attempt by the United States to develop an alternative approach to a global legally binding emissions reductions framework by focusing on clean technology cooperation among a select number of leading states, fade away after a few years.

The normalization of market and voluntary approaches to climate governance as a legitimate and appropriate response to the threat of climate change has, therefore, not been without contest. In particular, with the rise of carbon markets as a means of allowing wealthier countries to meet their emission reductions obligations, we have seen contestation over their consequences particularly for poorer communities whose resources (such as land and forests) become subject to an international trade in emission reductions (Chapter 2). This has resulted in instances of displacement and conflict that critics refer to as "carbon colonialism"[8] as local regimes of resource management are brought into the realm of global climate governance.[9] Likewise, Chapter 4 showed through the example of carbon forestry projects in Mexico how important local institutions are in ensuring that local communities can capture some of the benefits of engagement with the carbon economy. These examples suggest the importance of the link between the processes of governing climate change and the procedural and distributional aspects of climate governance: who participates and who decides exercises a powerful influence over who wins and who loses.

Consequences and contestations in climate governance

Amid such diversity among actors and practices of climate governance, it is difficult to form definitive judgments about what is working and for whom. One answer is that it is difficult to know in quantitative terms who is reducing by how much as more actors get involved in setting their standards employing different baselines and covering different GHG (as we saw in Chapter 5). As responsibility is diffused and governance tools proliferate, maintaining a clear view of what is being achieved overall is very difficult.[10] Symbolically, the fact that governments advance slowly towards a successor to the Kyoto Protocol, as we saw in Chapter 1, or the fact that many of the world's leading firms now endorse the idea of action of climate change, as we saw in Chapter 5, represents success on one level. Key actors are engaged and the momentum is there.

And yet, despite the enormous proliferation of initiatives aimed at reporting, benchmarking, and measuring performance, at funding projects and trading credits that we have seen throughout the book, it would be difficult to argue that the world is showing genuine progress in moving away from a model of development that is fuelling climate change. Continued emissions growth tells a different story. Economic growth and emissions trajectories of GHG continue to be closely aligned, and governments and corporations alike continue to scour the Earth for new sources of fossil fuels in spite of full knowledge of the human and ecological consequences of burning them into the atmosphere.[11] Rather than prioritize fundamental changes in production and consumption of energy, the world's most industrialized countries are seeking to locate the lowest cost ways of reducing emissions by identifying emission reduction projects in the global South, or to make more money by trading their way out of trouble through the buying and selling of emissions permits. We have seen how climate justice movements and critics of carbon trading in particular have sought to question the assumed efficiency and effectiveness of such market-based governance instruments as well as highlight the inequalities and injustices that they create or reinforce. But in a context of such power inequalities within and between societies, the means of holding to account those that benefit most from what has been called the "un-governance" of climate change by those that are or will suffer the worst consequences of inaction are often just not there.

One conclusion that can surely be drawn from the evidence presented in this book, however, is that the landscape of climate governance is ever-changing, and interesting and unpredictable alliances between actors, even former adversaries, are increasingly common. It is to be hoped that enough powerful allies in the world of finance and business can be brought on board alongside enough governments with the will and power to lead on action on climate change, and be pressured, cajoled, and shamed into action by an increasingly active public and civil society, to adequately address perhaps the greatest collective action problem the world currently faces.

Theoretical implications

How then are we to explain and make sense of the patterns of governance described above? In the Introduction we introduced some key themes and literatures that we believe are useful in explaining this complex tapestry of climate governance. Here, we gather some of the key insights that emerge from this book, having now examined a range of forms of climate governance.

If we accept that climate governance now takes place in many more places and is produced by a greater range of actors, it is clear that we need to adopt theoretical tools and concepts that allow us to go beyond the state as the primary focus of analysis. Emphasizing the role of non-state actors and explaining their influence on international climate policy is one important aspect of this.[12] But given that many of these actors are cooperating and working together in ways which bypass the climate regime altogether, we need to explore their roles as governance actors in ways that are not defined by whether and when they affect state policy. We saw in Chapter 3 how organizations such as the Climate Group have been able to bring together novel coalitions of cities, businesses, and civil society organizations to share and build on successful initiatives to reduce GHG emissions. An emphasis on networks that cut across national and international divisions is useful here.[13] We also saw how work on public–private partnerships can usefully be applied to governance innovation in the climate arena.[14] A key challenge that remains is how to account for the fact that some partnerships are more successful and more powerful than others.[15]

The political economy approaches that we discussed in the Introduction offer promising ways forward for looking at the relations of power that underpin political coalitions which seek to deliver or frustrate change.[16] They emphasize in particular the role of economic actors in the very processes which are subject to regulation, where powerful interests are at stake and from whence change ultimately has to come. By focusing on the dependencies and material and political alliances that bind together state, market, and civil society actors, they provide a sense of how much autonomy, "policy space," and scope for effective action they have.[17] This could be the developing country governments dependent on World Bank finance, or developed country governments reluctant to regulate the emissions of businesses that threaten to relocate their operations elsewhere. But it could also be the coalitions formed between financial capital in the city of London and NGOs pushing business to commit to action or conflicts between different business interests which create openings for change.[18] This provides us with a useful way to understand why climate is governed the way it is and on whose behalf, by placing power at the heart of governance analysis.

All of this implies broader understandings of power than have traditionally been used in the study of climate governance. Notions of "power over" and the ability to demand actions of others continue to be important: the power of states over firms and local authorities is critical to their ability to ensure they enforce actions on climate change. But many of the forms of private governance that we discussed in Chapters 3 and 5 show that even without sanctions, forms of peer and consumer or activist pressure often provide incentives for compliance.[19] We have also seen how power operates in more subtle ways, through the presentation of knowledge and the inclusion or exclusion of emphasis on some aspects of climate science and economics and not others. Appeals to moral authority are strongly made by developing countries and underpin NGO-led proposals on contraction and convergence or the greenhouse development rights framework that was discussed in Chapter 1. Considering power in these terms means understanding how it works through discourse and in the everyday practice of policies and actions to address climate change.

The power that actors wield in climate governance is not just visible within the self-proclaimed arenas of climate policy, nor does it derive primarily from the power they wield in that area, however. As Susan Strange argues in her critique of regime theories of international governance:

since the chain of cause and effect so often originates in technology and markets, passing through national policy decisions to emerge as negotiating postures in multilateral discussions, it follows that attention to the resultant international agreement of some sort is apt to overlook most of the determining factors on which agreement may, in brief, rest.[20]

Likewise, the World Bank is an increasingly central actor in climate governance, not primarily because of its Climate Investment Funds but because it exerts such influence over the overall development strategies of so many developing countries. Separating its role as the world's largest lender from its role as one among many actors in climate governance makes little sense, because how developing countries engage with it as a climate actor is shaped by the knowledge of the power the institution wields over so many other aspects of their economies.

Climate governance is ironically both a microcosm of a larger global political economy, but also a meta feature of that system in so far as virtually all areas of political activity have an impact on or might be understood as forms of climate governance. For instance, the WTO or the World Bank would not consider themselves environmental organizations or climate agencies, but the mandates they have and the influence they wield mean they have a tremendous impact on the level of GHG emissions that pass into the atmosphere. Trade agreements that mean goods are transported over larger distances and financial loans for coal-fired power stations in the case of the World Bank make the work of the official climate regime that much harder. Ultimately, whether we have the collective capacity and will to address climate change in the time frames available to avoid its most dangerous consequences will depend on fundamental change in policy areas beyond the direct control of many of the actors and initiatives that we have explored in this book.

Last but not least, the examples throughout this book of governance in practice suggest it takes on a much broader range of forms in reality than many theoretical accounts allow for. We have clearly observed, as others have done in other areas, a shift from government to governance in which more actors are involved in processes of governing.[21] The tools of governance have also broadened from law and regulation to voluntary standards, codes, and partnerships, but also day-to-day supply chain management within firms whose decisions often dwarf those made in the traditional arenas of climate governance in terms of their impact on emissions of GHG. Whilst the tremendous diversity and dynamism of climate governance generates huge challenges of coordination, accountability, and effectiveness, a fact which in itself makes it hard to get a handle on how effective action is and who is benefiting, the plurality of sites of action could also be a positive thing as actors move between arenas trying to advance action in the fastest and most effective way they can, working with whom they need to, wherever that happens to be. We surely have to hope for all our sakes that the forms of climate governance we are now busy constructing are up to the scale of the challenge we are faced with and can deliver change within the time we have available to us to prevent the very worst scenarios of uncontrolled climate change.

Notes

1 Back issues of *Earth Negotiations Bulletin* are available online at http://www. iisd.ca/voltoc.html [accessed January 21, 2015].

2 Matthew Hoffman, *Climate Governance at the Crossroads: Experimenting with a Global Response after Kyoto* (Oxford: Oxford University Press, 2011).

3 ICTSD, "China to End Challenged Subsidies in Wind Power Case," *Bridges Trade BioRes* June 13, 2011, available online at http://www.ictsd.org/bridges-news/biores/news/china-to-end-challenged-subsidies-in-wind-power-case [accessed January 21, 2015].

4 David Levy, "Business and the Evolution of the Climate Regime: The Dynamics of Corporate Strategies," in *The Business of Global Environmental Governance,* eds David Levy and Peter Newell (Cambridge, Mass.: MIT Press, 2005): 73–105.

5 Michael Lipskey, *Street-level Bureaucracy* (New York: Russell Sage Foundation, 1983).

6 The World Mayors and Local Governments Climate Protection Agreement, available online at http://archive.iclei.org/index.php?id=10395 [accessed January 21, 2015].

7 Peter Newell, Phillip Pattberg, and Heike Schroeder, "Multi-actor Governance and the Environment," *Annual Review of Environment and Resources* 37 (2012): 365–87.

8 Heidi Bachram, "Climate Fraud and Carbon Colonialism: The New Trade in Greenhouse Gases," *Capitalism, Nature, Socialism* 15, no. 4 (2004): 5–20.

9 Peter Newell and Adam Bumpus, "The Global Political Ecology of the CDM," *Global Environmental Politics* 12, no. 4 (2012): 49–68.

10 Harriet Bulkeley, Liliana Andonova, Karin Bäckstrand, Michele Betsill, Daniel Compagnon, Rosaleen Duffy, Ans Kolk, Matthew Hoffmann, David Levy, Peter Newell, Tori Milledge, Matthew Paterson, Philipp Pattberg, Stacy VanDeveer, "Governing Climate Change Transnationally: Assessing the Evidence from a Database of Sixty Initiatives," *Environment and Planning C: Government and Policy* 30, no. 4 (2012): 591–612.

11 Greenpeace International, *Point of No Return: The Massive Climate Threats We Must Avoid* (Amsterdam: Greenpeace International, 2013).

12 Bas Arts, "Non-State Actors in Global Environmental Governance: New Arrangements Beyond the State," in *New Modes of Governance in the Global System: Exploring Publicness, Delegation and Inclusiveness*, eds Mathias Koenig-Archibugi and Michael Zürn (Basingstoke, UK: Palgrave, 2006): 177–201; Peter Newell, *Climate for Change: Non-State Actors and the Global Politics of the Greenhouse* (Cambridge: Cambridge University Press, 2000); Michelle Betsill and Elizabeth Correll, "NGO Influence in International Environmental Negotiations: A Framework for Analysis," *Global Environmental Politics* 1, no. 4 (2001): 65–85.

13 Harriet Bulkeley, "Reconfiguring Environmental Governance: Towards a Politics of Scales and Networks," *Political Geography* 24 (2005): 875–902.

14 Karin Backstränd and Charlotte Streck, "New Partnerships in Global Environmental Policy: the Clean Development Mechanism," *Journal of Environment and Development* 13, no. 3 (2004): 295–322.

15 Phillip Pattberg, "Public–private Partnerships in Global Climate Governance," *WIREs Climate Change* 1, no. 2 (2010): 279–87.

16 Jonas Meckling, *Carbon Coalitions* (Cambridge, Mass.: MIT Press, 2011).

17 Kevin Gallagher, ed., *Putting Development First* (London: Zed Books, 2005).

18 Peter Newell and Matthew Paterson, *Climate Capitalism* (Cambridge: Cambridge University Press, 2010).

19 Peter Newell, "Civil Society, Corporate Accountability and the Politics of Climate Change," *Global Environmental Politics* 8, no. 3 (2008): 124–55.

20 Susan Strange, "Cave! Hic Dragones: A Critique of Regime Analysis," *International Organization* 36, no. 2 (1983): 488–90.

21 James Rosenau and Ernst Otto Czempiel, eds, *Governance Without Government: Order and Change in World Politics* (Cambridge: Cambridge University Press, 1992); Vasudha Chhotray and Gerry Stoker, *Governance Theory: A Cross-Disciplinary Approach* (Basingstoke, UK: Palgrave Macmillan, 2008); Rod A. W. Rhodes, "The New Governance: Governing Without Government," *Political Studies* 44, no. 4 (1996): 652–67.

SELECT BIBLIOGRAPHY

For more on theoretical approaches to climate governance and environmental governance in general (Chapter 1), see:

Bulkeley, H. "Reconfiguring Environmental Governance: Towards a Politics of Scales and Networks," *Political Geography* 24, no. 8 (2005): 875–902. Discusses the ways in which assumptions about scale and space in political analyses affect our understanding of the processes of governance.

Newell, P. *Climate for Change: Non-state Actors and the global politics of the greenhouse* (Cambridge: Cambridge University Press, 2000). Provides an assessment and explanation of the political influence of a range of non-state actors (the scientific community, mass media, business groups, and environmental NGOs) upon the climate regime up to Kyoto.

—"The Political Economy of Global Environmental Governance," *Review of International Studies* 34 (July 2008): 507–29. Constructs a political economy framework for addressing key questions in environmental governance about who governs and how, what is to be governed (and what is not), and on whose behalf.

Okereke, C., Bulkeley, H., and Schroeder, H. "Conceptualizing Climate Governance Beyond the International Regime," *Global Environmental Politics* 9, no. 1 (2009): 58–78. Examines the strengths and weaknesses of regime approaches and global governance perspectives in understanding the governance of climate change, and assesses the potential contribution of neo-Gramscian and Foucauldian theory for such an analysis.

Paterson, M. *Global Warming, Global Politics* (London: Routledge, 1996). Assesses different strands of international relations theory in terms of their ability to explain processes of international cooperation around the UNFCCC.

For more on the history of the climate negotiations and the evolving nature of the climate regime (Chapter 2), see:

Biermann, F., Pattberg, P., and Zelli, F. eds, *Global Climate Governance Beyond 2012* (Cambridge: Cambridge University Press, 2010). Explores issues of architecture, agency, and adaptation in the climate regime.

Grubb, M., Vrolijk, C., and Brack, D. *The Kyoto Protocol: A Guide and Assessment* (London: RIIA, 1999). Provides a useful assessment of the key features of the Kyoto Protocol and the negotiations that preceded it.

Hoffman, M. *Climate Governance at the Crossroads: Experimenting with a Global Response After Kyoto* (Oxford: Oxford University Press, 2011). Examines the breakdown of the "mega multilateralism" of the international negotiations process and new sites and forms of climate governance emerging "beyond" the state.

Mintzer, I., and Leonard, J. A. eds, *Negotiating Climate Change: The Inside Story of the Rio Convention* (Cambridge: Cambridge University Press, 1994). Highlights the perspectives of leading state and non-state actors on the negotiations that led to the UNFCCC.

For more on the North–South politics of climate change and issues of equity (Chapter 3), see:

Adger, N., Paavola, J., Huq, S., and Mace, M. J. eds, *Fairness in Adaptation to Climate Change* (Cambridge, Mass.: MIT Press, 2006). Explores the importance of issues of equity, justice, and fairness in adapting to the effects of climate change.

Roberts, J. T., and Parks, B. *Climate of Injustice: Global Inequality, North–South Politics and Climate Policy* (Cambridge, Mass.: MIT Press, 2007). Shows how North–South conflicts in the climate negotiations are a feature of broader historical inequities between developed and less-developed countries.

UNDP, *Human Development Report: Fighting Climate Change—Human Solidarity in a Divided World* (New York: Oxford University Press, 2007/8). Takes a systematic look at the developmental aspects of efforts to tackle climate change, with a strong emphasis on issues of rights, justice, and historical responsibility.

For more on transnational governance networks and the role of community in climate governance (Chapters 4 and 5), see:

Andonova, L., Betsill, M., and Bulkeley, H., "Transnational Climate Governance," *Global Environmental Politics* 9, no. 2 (May 2009): 52–73. Examines the origins and nature of transnational governance in relation to climate change and develops a typology for analyzing transnational governance initiatives.

Bulkeley, H., Andonova, L., Betsill, M., Compagnon, D., Hoffman, M., Hale, T., Newell, P., Paterson, M., Rogers, C., and Vanderveer, S., *Transnational Climate Change Governance* (Cambridge: Cambridge University Press, 2014). The first comprehensive assessment of the transnational climate governance phenomenon, analyzing a database of 60 case studies and developing new conceptual perspectives through which to evaluate this phenomenon.

Walker, G., and Devine-Wright, P. "Community Renewable Energy: What Does it Mean?" *Energy Policy* 36, no. 2 (2008): 498–99. Examines the ways in which communities have been mobilized to participate in climate governance through renewable energy projects.

For more on business responses to climate change and ways of understanding the role of business as an actor in climate governance (Chapter 6), see:

Begg, K., van der Woerd, F., and Levy, D. eds, *The Business of Climate Change* (Sheffield, UK: Greenleaf Publishing, 2005). Provides a range of sectoral and country-based case studies of business responses to climate change.

Meckling, J. *Carbon Coalitions: Business, Climate Politics and the Rise of Emissions Trading* (Cambridge, Mass.: MIT Press, 2011). Analyzes the formation of a transnational coalition of businesses and NGOs around support for international emissions trading as a key policy response to climate change.

Pulver, S. "Making Sense of Corporate Environmentalism: An Environmental Contestation Approach to Analyzing the Causes and Consequences of the Climate Change Policy Split in the Oil Industry," *Organization and Environment* 20, no. 1 (2007): 44–83. Looks at the origins of divergent corporate strategies in the oil industry with respect to climate change, and the implications of this for business responses to the issue.

INDEX

ROUTLEDGE GLOBAL INSTITUTIONS SERIES

Books currently under contract include:

The Regional Development Banks
Lending with a regional flavor
by Jonathan R. Strand (University of Nevada)

Millennium Development Goals (MDGs)
For a people-centered development agenda?
by Sakiko Fukada-Parr (The New School)

The Bank for International Settlements
The politics of global financial supervision in the age of high finance
by Kevin Ozgercin (SUNY College at Old Westbury)

International Migration
by Khalid Koser (Geneva Centre for Security Policy)

Human Development
by Richard Ponzio

The International Monetary Fund (2nd edition)
Politics of conditional lending
by James Raymond Vreeland (Georgetown University)

The UN Global Compact
by Catia Gregoratti (Lund University)

Institutions for Women's Rights
by Charlotte Patton (York College, CUNY) and Carolyn Stephenson (University of Hawaii)

International Aid
by Paul Mosley (University of Sheffield)

Global Consumer Policy
by Karsten Ronit (University of Copenhagen)

The Changing Political Map of Global Governance
by Anthony Payne (University of Sheffield) and Stephen Robert Buzdugan (Manchester Metropolitan University)

Coping with Nuclear Weapons
by W. Pal Sidhu

Global Governance and China
The dragon's learning curve
edited by Scott Kennedy (Indiana University)

The Politics of Global Economic Surveillance
by Martin S. Edwards (Seton Hall University)

Mercy and Mercenaries
Humanitarian agencies and private security companies
by Peter Hoffman

Regional Organizations in the Middle East
by James Worrall (University of Leeds)

Reforming the UN Development System
The politics of incrementalism
by Silke Weinlich (Duisburg-Essen University)

The United Nations as a Knowledge Organization
by Nanette Svenson (Tulane University)

The International Criminal Court
The politics and practice of prosecuting atrocity crimes
by Martin Mennecke (University of Copenhagen)

The Politics of International Organizations
Views from insiders
edited by Patrick Weller (Griffith University) and Xu Yi-chong (Griffith University)

The African Union (2nd edition)
Challenges of globalization, security, and governance
by Samuel M. Makinda (Murdoch University), F. Wafula Okumu (African Union), and David Mickler (University of Western Australia)

BRICS
by João Pontes Nogueira (Catholic University, Rio de Janeiro) and Monica Herz (Catholic University, Rio de Janeiro)

Expert Knowledge in Global Trade
edited by Erin Hannah (University of Western Ontario), James Scott (University of Manchester), and Silke Trommer (Murdoch University)

The European Union (2nd edition)
Clive Archer (Manchester Metropolitan University)

Governing Climate Change (2nd edition)
Harriet A. Bulkeley (Durham University) and Peter Newell (University of East Anglia)

Contemporary Human Rights Ideas (2nd edition)
Betrand Ramcharan (Geneva Graduate Institute of International and Development Studies)

Protecting the Internally Displaced
Rhetoric and reality
Phil Orchard (University of Queensland)

The Arctic Council
Within the far North
Douglas C. Nord (Umea University)

Past as Prelude?
Wartime history and the future United Nations
edited by Dan Plesch (SOAS, University of London) and Thomas G. Weiss (CUNY Graduate Center)

For further information regarding the series, please contact:
Nicola Parkin, Editor, Politics & International Studies
Taylor & Francis
2 Park Square, Milton Park, Abingdon
Oxford OX14 4RN, UK
nicola.parkin@tandf.co.uk
www.routledge.com